GO YOUR OWN WAY

BEN GROUNDWATER

Hardie Grant

TRAVEL

CONTENTS

Paragliders (the writer
included) fly high above
Interlaken, Switzerland

INTRODUCTION

YOU CAN DO THIS

You can do anything.

That's the key point to remember, the mantra to regularly repeat. In fact it's probably the most important thing of all. Because there will be difficulties on this grand solo journey you're about to set out on. You will find yourself lost in the strangest of places. You will become stuck in the stickiest of situations. There will be times on your travels when you might feel lonely, or confused, or homesick, or just plain bored. You may even wonder if this whole thing really was such a great idea after all.

But you can do this. You are ready, right now, to travel the world alone. You already possess the skills, you already have the courage and the confidence, even if you don't yet know it. There is so much more in you than you ever would have believed, and it will all be revealed when you decide to tackle this planet with no one but yourself to rely on. You won't just survive out there; you'll thrive. You'll come to love this pursuit. You'll hunger for it when you're back at home. You'll want to do it again and again.

Solo travel isn't a punishment after all – it's a joy. It's empowering. It's a bold and courageous move that will change your life completely. It's the chance to conquer the fears that may have held you back and enjoy the adventures you've always dreamed of. This journey will teach you about the world and the diverse group of personalities that inhabits it, but more importantly it will teach you about yourself: about everything you're capable of, the very things you may have doubted when you first stepped on the plane.

Solo travel is the ultimate freedom, the ultimate power. It's about going to the places you want to go to, doing the things you want to do, seeing and feeling and tasting and experiencing the world in a way that suits only you. It may sound like a solitary pursuit, but really, it's anything but. To travel on your own is to meet an endless cast of characters: new friends and partners in crime, some of whom will be gone almost as soon as they appeared, and some who may be with you for a lifetime.

So let's answer that big question, the one that might still be hanging over you, the one that might be stopping you from clicking *confirm* on that air ticket and following your dreams to foreign and exotic lands that offer so much thrill and adventure.

Can you do this?

Can you travel the world on your own? Can you take it all on by yourself?

Yes. Without a shadow of a doubt. And now is the time to begin. ●

**It was a matter of hours before
I made my first friend.**

Son was a Vietnamese guy, probably a few years younger than me, with an open, friendly face, and an easygoing way about him. I couldn't believe my luck. Just three hours on my own in Hanoi and I'd already met someone, a local, someone I could chat to and hang out with and maybe get to know. What were the chances?

He'd approached me while I was sitting down by Hoan Kiem Lake, trying to adjust to new surroundings, to take it all in. He was a student who wanted to practise his English, he said. I was a traveller who wanted to meet locals. It was ideal.

We chatted for a while, Son and I, until he mentioned he was keen to grab some lunch and would be happy to show me a little of his city, to share his culture, if I'd like. I was 100 per cent on board. This was my first-ever solo journey, my first-ever trip to

Asia, and I wanted to open myself up to the world. I wanted to not think, but to do, to follow my gut, to have experiences, to create stories.

And, besides, Son had a great idea: he wanted to introduce me to something a little different. Most tourists don't know this, he said, but snake meat is a delicacy in Vietnam. We could try it if I wanted. Yeah, I wanted. So the two of us jumped in the back of a cab and made our way through the city, crossing a river, watching as the high-rises of central Hanoi began to fade in the car's mirrors, as the traffic thinned and we hit the outskirts of town.

Eventually we pulled up at a nondescript restaurant on a dusty old street, somewhere so far from anything I'd ever known or could understand that it would have been frightening if I wasn't so excited.

We sat down, and Son explained the menu. We could have a big snake or a small snake, he said. And it would be alive. The owner would kill the reptile in front of us: would skin it, drain its blood and butcher it.

This gave me pause. I'm up for new things, I thought. I want to try authentic experiences. But maybe I'm not ready – on my first day, in the first few hours of my trip – for freshly slaughtered snake.

'Do they, um, have any pre-prepared snake?' I asked. 'Something smaller?'

Sure, Son said. We could have snake spring rolls. We could drink a few shots of snake whisky. Cool, I said. Deal. So the two of us sat there in that restaurant in who knows where, trading stories, drinking shots of whisky and eating our snake spring rolls. I was loving it, just lapping it all up, still not quite able to believe my luck, how this had all fallen in my lap, how I'd taken the chance to see the world on my own and already the world was repaying me.

That is, until the bill arrived. And then it was my turn to pay. I realised, at that moment, that I hadn't seen a menu at any point. I hadn't thought to ask how much this would cost. Everything was cheap in Vietnam, after all. There was no need to enquire – meals cost a couple of dollars, tops.

But not this meal. I was passed a slip of paper: *US$100*. One hundred dollars! That was my total weekly budget. A month's worth of food. It was a huge amount of money. And worse than the horror of the bill: the realisation that my 'friend' had been taking me for a ride, that I wasn't special, or lucky, at all. I was a total chump. Son had spotted a sucker from a mile away. I might as well have had the word stamped on my forehead.

I argued half-heartedly from a place of extreme weakness: I was miles out of town, alone, with no idea of how to get back to my hostel. I said it was crazy; they said this is how much snake costs. It's special, they said. It's endangered. *Ah, great*. I said I didn't have $100. Who would? They said fine, just give us whatever you have. I had $70. They said it would do.

I walked out of the restaurant stunned: it had all been so easy; it had all gone so wrong. Son and I jumped on a motorbike taxi and made our way back into town, back to my hostel, back to a place I kind of knew. Son was still chattering away, acting as if nothing was up. I was still too surprised to say anything, still shocked by how it had all gone down. As we pulled up by the hostel I got off and slipped Son even more money – a few notes to cover the taxi. I made to leave, wallet empty, shoulders slumped.

Son smiled. 'Hey,' he said. 'What are you doing for lunch tomorrow?' ●

Sink or swim.

That's how it works for solo travellers. And we all, eventually, swim. You make mistakes when you travel by yourself. Maybe you'll spend far more money than you should. Maybe you'll go somewhere you really shouldn't. Maybe you'll get on the wrong bus or turn up at the wrong hostel or place your trust in someone who doesn't deserve it. These errors are all part of the solo travel experience. They're part of what will make you a stronger, smarter, more resilient person.

I hold no grudge against Son. He was just a guy, trying to make his way in the world. I mean, sure, he chose to do that by swindling dumb tourists out of their money, which isn't ideal. But my brush with him did help transform me from one of those dumb tourists into someone a little wiser: a total bargain at $70, when you think about it. And, anyway, travel is all about the stories. Solo travel, in particular. See the world on your own and you'll end up with plenty of anecdotes, some of which will feature you as the hero, some the idiot. That's fine. Travel has a way of levelling things out.

That's not to say that I set out on that first solo journey intending to collect stories I could retell. I wasn't in it back then for pure personal transformation either, or for any sort of educational experience. I was there for the same reason many solo travellers find themselves seeing the world alone: necessity. Sometimes you simply don't have anyone else to go with.

If that's a factor behind your decision to take off solo, then fear not: it's a perfectly acceptable one. Sometimes no one you know wants to do the things you want to do. It's that simple. Maybe you've just finished school or university, or quit your job or broken up with your partner, and you want to have all of those amazing experiences you always dreamed of, but no one else is in the same place. Or maybe you're tired of compromising, of travelling the way other people want you to, of giving up your time to do things someone else's way in the hope they'll reciprocate.

Those reasons to head out there on your own are as good as any, and they certainly played a part in my decision to take that first solo trip. I just had no one else to travel with. I was in my early twenties, I'd recently come out of a five-year relationship, my job was good but was probably going nowhere. I felt the time was right to get out and see the world. No one I knew was in that same place, so I went alone.

The unforgettable entrance to the Treasury in Petra, Jordan

I've been travelling solo now for about 15 years. I've been to dozens of countries, to uncountable cities across every continent. I've had good times and I've had bad; I've made crazy mistakes and got myself into all sorts of ridiculous situations, and then eventually found my way out. And I've come to love this pursuit, to appreciate everything going solo can bring to the travel experience. I've found small annoyances – there's no one to watch your backpack when you need to go to the toilet, and you can't order as many things at a restaurant – but mostly I've gloried in the freedom that solo travel brings. I've loved the chance to meet people and make my own decisions, to challenge myself and discover what I'm capable of.

It's hugely exciting to decide that you don't need anyone else to make your dream come true. Admittedly, it's also intimidating. There's no one else to blame when things go wrong. It's all on you. That's a lot of responsibility to shoulder. There's also, however, no one else to please, no one else to keep happy. Solo travel is the ultimate freedom. You get to visit whichever places you want, stay wherever you want, eat whatever you want, do and see whatever you want, and drop everything whenever you feel like it to go do something else.

You can do anything, and you can *be* anything. No one knows you. You can completely reinvent yourself if you feel like it. Or you can become a slightly different version of yourself: more confident, more spontaneous, braver. Whatever feels authentic, whatever feels comfortable – that's who you can be.

You might be worried about being lonely on your travels, and it's true, there will be moments when you miss having company. You might feel the strange sensation of being alone in a city of millions, of being isolated among huge crowds. That's normal; it's part of the experience. The thing to remember is that this feeling will pass, because there are just so many people out there to meet: not only locals but fellow travellers too, solo adventurers who are feeling exactly the same things as you, and who will welcome the chance to meet a kindred spirit.

You generally won't have to put in much effort to meet these people, either – friends come to you when you're travelling. Stay in a hostel and company will walk into your dorm room every day. Potential travel buddies will hang around in the shared kitchen. They'll lounge on the couches. Travellers are just about the friendliest group of people around, and most of them are looking for a partner in crime. They want someone to share their experience, too.

In other words, you'll very rarely be lonely if you don't want to be.

You meet a lot of people out there on the road who will influence you in one way or another. Some might change your day; others might change your mood. Some, meanwhile, will change your entire life. But here's the best part: the time you spend with these people and the paths they take you on are entirely up to you. When you decide to part ways with them, when you've learnt what you need to learn and experienced what you want to experience (or when the Ed Sheeran wannabe you've been hanging out with plays his guitar one too many times), you can just head off on your own. You can pack up your things, say goodbye and move on to the next place, the next adventure, the next group of new friends.

It might take a while to find them, but that's okay, because you can handle this on your own. You can do anything. ●

Left: Barcelona's charming streets

Bottom: A meerkat perches on a safari-goer's head in the Makgadikgadi Salt Pan, Botswana

... you'll very rarely be lonely if you don't want to be.

13 lessons every solo traveller learns.

It's a big world out there. A scary world, sometimes. A world filled with dodgy taxi drivers and bad food, dirty hostels and shady locals. When you first step out on your own it can be a little daunting, but as time goes by and you settle into the travel scene, you will very quickly come to love it. And that's because every traveller learns certain lessons – about themselves, about travel and about the world in general. Lessons like these.

YOU CAN GET USED TO PRETTY MUCH ANYTHING IN ABOUT THREE DAYS

Every time I go camping, or stay in a hostel, or even eat questionable street food, the feeling on that first day is the same: *urgh*. I can't get clean. There are people making noise in my room. This food is going to poison me. But after about three days of anything – any level of discomfort, of grot or grime – you just get used to it. And then it becomes fun.

YOU CAN SURVIVE WITH LESS FOOD AND LESS SLEEP THAN YOU THOUGHT

Couldn't find anywhere to have breakfast this morning? No worries. Stayed up all night boozing and now you have to catch a bus? That's alright. Blew your budget on a dumb souvenir and now you have to survive on packet noodles? No dramas. You can survive.

YOUR VERSION OF GROTTY IS NOT REALLY GROTTY

What you may have once thought was incredibly disgusting – showering in a mouldy bathroom, drying yourself with the gross hostel towel, wearing the same T-shirt four days in a row, never washing your socks – becomes kind of run-of-the-mill once you've been travelling solo for a couple of months.

YOU WILL NOT GET ROBBED (ALTHOUGH MAYBE YOU WILL)

First-time solo travellers tend to obsess over security, but after a while you realise that the world isn't actually out to get you, and if you just take a few easy precautions the odds are high that you won't get robbed while you travel. (Although you still might, so don't carry anything you can't bear to lose.)

EATING BY YOURSELF IS OKAY

It feels weird to begin with, going into a restaurant and asking for a table for one. You feel uncomfortable. You don't know what to do. Read a book? Listen to music? Write in your journal? It takes a while to realise that, sure, you can do any of those things if you want. Or you can just sit there and watch the world go by and enjoy your food. Eating alone is really no big deal.

AIR TRAVEL IS CONVENIENT, TRAIN TRAVEL IS ROMANTIC, AND BUS TRAVEL SUCKS

An aeroplane will get you there quickly, but it's not much fun. On a train you get to meet people, you can often dine at a proper restaurant, and you watch the world go past your window. And on a bus ... Well, you'll get where you need to go. Eventually. Probably.

YOU'LL NEED FAR MORE MONEY THAN YOU THOUGHT

List all the money you'll spend on flights and transfers, and accommodation, and food, and drinks, and souvenirs, and insurance, and all of the various costs that will pop up on your overseas adventure. Tally all of that up, arrive at your total – and then double it.

THE FIRST PRICE IS NEVER THE RIGHT PRICE

This holds true for any object that isn't clearly labelled with a price. While haggling doesn't come naturally to everyone, it's something you have to get used to if you don't want to be ripped off over and over again.

PATIENCE IS A VIRTUE

Things go wrong when you travel by yourself. Lots of things. The train is late, the hotel has lost your booking, and you can feel a rumble in your stomach that means last night's street food was a bad choice. But you have to roll with the punches when you travel, or you'll quickly go insane.

ALL UNDERWEAR IS TWO-SIDED

Desperate times call for desperate measures. You'll come to value this.

ALWAYS – ALWAYS – REMEMBER TO BOOK AN AISLE OR A WINDOW SEAT

Unless you fancy spending 14 hours locked in a battle for armrest space with the two hulks sitting either side of you, make sure you book an aisle seat or a window when you pay for that ticket.

SOMEWHERE, AT SOME TIME, SOMEONE WILL SUCCESSFULLY RIP YOU OFF

There's no point getting too upset about this. These people are professionals; they make a living, sadly, from taking tourists for a ride. It'll most likely happen when you've just arrived somewhere, when you're jet-lagged and tired and maybe experiencing some culture shock. You will get ripped off. And you won't be the first, or the last.

YOU'RE FAR MORE RESOURCEFUL THAN YOU THINK

This. This is the number-one thing every traveller realises. You might have thought you're terrible with directions, or that you'd struggle with the language barrier and wouldn't cope in a crisis, but once you throw yourself in the deep end and have to survive on your own in the world, you'll come to know: you're far better at this stuff than you ever realised.

CHAPTER ONE

HOW TO PLAN YOUR TRIP

Opposite top: A good camera is every solo traveller's best friend

Opposite bottom: When it comes to packing – take everything you think you'll need, and halve it

Top left: Sometimes the planning is just as fun as the execution

Top right: First check – ensure your passport is up to date

Bottom: There's always time to keep a diary when you travel solo

It might have been Namibia where I met Kosta.

Or maybe it was South Africa. I'm not sure. After three months on an overland truck tour you start to lose track of which country you're in – the roads and campsites and faces all blur into one another. Still, I remember what became of our encounter.

It was a chance meeting, one of hundreds I had on that African adventure. You meet new people every day on a trip like that: you chat, get to know them for a few hours and then you wave goodbye, consigning them to memory. The campsite, I remember, was a dusty one, a remote place with a clearing for tents, a dodgy little bar and not much else. It was a stopover point in the perfect centre of nowhere.

I'd finished setting up my tent, hammering pegs into hard ground, and figured I could use a cold Windhoek beer as the sun went down. That's when I met Kosta. He'd come in with another group, in a different truck, and had apparently had the same post-pitching idea. So there we were, two travellers striking up a conversation at a one-horse African campsite bar. We established that we were both Australian, both on holidays, and then swapped the usual chat about what we did for a living back in the real world.

I was a journalist on sabbatical, I told him, taking a quarter-life-crisis gap year to escape the seriousness of a career. He was a Europe-based bus driver for the tour company Topdeck, spending his off-season on holidays with someone else at the wheel.

'What are you going to do after Africa?' Kosta asked.

'I dunno,' I said. 'I guess I'll head to London to try to find a job. Or maybe I'll go to Edinburgh. Or … somewhere else.'

'Why don't you come work for Topdeck? You could be a cook for us, easily.'

'Really?' I kind of laughed, then went back to drinking my Windhoek and talking about who'd made the footy finals back home.

Travel provides you with an infinite number of chance encounters that can change your plans, and your life.

But Kosta's idea stuck like an acacia thorn. We went our separate ways the following morning but for the next couple of weeks, as my tour drew to an end, the prospect of a summer on a bus in Europe became more and more attractive, until I finally sent an email to the contact Kosta had given me.

And you know what? He was right. I could become a cook. Easily. A few months later I was on a bus in France, in training; a couple of weeks after that I was working on my first tour. For someone who'd had no plan and no idea, it was the dream outcome. Over the next six months that job would take me sailing in Greece and motor-yacht cruising in Croatia. It would send me running with bulls in Pamplona and drinking with locals in Munich. I would serve eight banquets in the shadow of the Eiffel Tower. I would go on seven booze cruises in the Amsterdam canals. And all because of that chance meeting.

This is the thing with travel, particularly when you do it on your own: you meet so many people. Far more than you ever would at home. Travel provides you with an infinite number of chance encounters that can change your plans, and your life. This one certainly did, for me.

Pretty much every amazing thing that's happened to me since that trip has been part of the butterfly effect of that meeting in Namibia. Or South Africa. Or wherever it was. Where I've lived, the jobs I've worked, the people I've loved, the things I've seen – they all had something to do with that afternoon with Kosta. Of course, I've also had thousands of encounters with people that have amounted to absolutely nothing, but it only takes that one stroke of luck to change everything. The secret is to leave yourself open to these random offerings, to be able to recognise something new and something amazing and have the space to accept it.

And then to just drop everything and go. ●

You're on board now; you're doing this.

You've decided to travel solo, to go out and see the world by yourself, to take this on with no one to help. And to that I say, bravo. You won't regret it. Now it's time to plan. It's time to put aside all of the empowerment and inspiration for a second, and focus on the practicalities. Solo travel takes work, particularly in the planning stages. There's no one to share the load, no one to delegate the hard jobs to. This one's on you.

The first step to planning a solo trip is to figure out your itinerary. It's also worth bearing in mind, as the story on the previous page shows, that while it's great to have your journey mapped out, it's also worth leaving yourself room to be flexible, to take up chances as they present themselves, as they inevitably will. Book flights, sure, and some accommodation. It's a great idea to have at least your first night or two planned for every destination. However, the secret to solo travel is to leave yourself space, both in a practical sense and a more abstract, mental sense, to drop everything and go with your gut if something exciting should come your way.

Before any of that can take place, though, you need to figure out where you're going. The second half of this book focuses on a few of my favourite places, and favourite journeys, to tackle on your own. Once you have a destination in mind, there's plenty more that can be done from the comfort of home before you begin this grand adventure.

FIGURE OUT YOUR ITINERARY

You need to strike a balance here, to plan but not overplan, to book but not get locked in. Everyone will have a personal threshold for these things, but in general you will at least want to get your flights booked: this is usually the biggest expense for any holiday, and it's the sort of thing that will only get more expensive the longer you leave it. So choose your destinations, choose your dates, and get those big international transfers locked down.

The next thing to think about is accommodation. As I mentioned, I've always found it handy to have at least one or two nights booked for any new city I happen to be turning up in. That way you avoid schlepping around town with all of your luggage, trying to find a place to stay, at the mercy of touts, and making decisions without consulting reviews or guidebooks. It only takes a small amount of effort to research each city and find the area you're most likely to want to be based, and book a few nights in a decent spot. From there, you can explore with ease and change your base if you need to. You're also free to leave the city entirely if you don't like it and another option comes up.

Though you can probably wait until you're on the ground to book things like intercity transfers and individual attractions, it's worth checking out how popular these options are, and how far in advance they'll need to be booked to ensure you get a spot. Some

attractions, particularly in Europe – for example, La Sagrada Família, the famous Gaudí church in Barcelona – are far cheaper and easier to access if you book online in advance.

FIGURE OUT YOUR STYLE OF TRAVEL

Just because you're travelling solo doesn't mean you have to be alone. A great way to ease into the solo travel experience is by doing a tour, giving yourself an instant bunch of travel buddies and the services of a guide to help you through any tricky spots. This allows you to find your feet on that first big outing, and it's also perfect for those who don't have the time or the inclination to do a lot of research and planning before their trip. Head out on a tour and someone has already done the hard work for you; you just have to turn up and enjoy.

The trick to getting it right is to choose a tour and a tour company that will match your personality, your budget and your travel desires. Companies such as Contiki and Topdeck run tours around the world aimed at young travellers, and these days they're more about culture than pure boozing, as some people might expect. The likes of Intrepid and G Adventures, meanwhile, offer even more of a cultural window into a destination, and their groups are smaller, which means less of a party and more of a personal experience. There are also plenty of destination-specific tour companies that are worth looking into, depending on where you decide to go.

... go with your gut if something exciting should come your way.

Touring is your safety net. If you decide you'd rather go without that safety net, though, that's also totally fine. It is, however, worth looking into small tours that go for a day or an evening in your chosen destination, as a way to get to know the place a little better and meet fellow travellers while you're doing it. Urban Adventures has some great options around the world.

CHOOSE YOUR ACCOMMODATION

Solo travellers, particularly those on a tight budget, have more choice than ever these days when it comes to their style of accommodation. The obvious option is a hostel, which offers plenty of advantages for those travelling on their own: shared accommodation, in the form of dorm rooms, keeps costs as low as possible; hostels are a social environment with plenty of avenues for meeting fellow travellers; and most good hostels also have travel desks that can help you plan and book any onward journeys. If you're after a little more privacy and have slightly more money to spend, many hostels also offer private rooms with ensuite bathrooms, and still allow access to shared kitchens and other social areas.

There are other options, though. The website Airbnb and its competitors offer the chance to rent a room in a local's house or apartment, meaning you have not only a place to stay but instant access to local life. For an even cheaper version, become a member of the website Couchsurfing, and you'll be able to sleep in spare rooms and on couches the world over for free. Couchsurfing hosts are often fellow travellers who are keen to meet new people and return the favour for free nights they've spent abroad.

START BOOKING

Booking in all of these elements – your flights, your tours, your accommodation – is easy to do before you leave, even without the use of a travel agent. Plenty of online portals exist to facilitate these bookings, helping you find the best prices and the best times to travel. Take a look at the handy references (see p. 248) for a list of websites that will help you get everything locked in.

Opposite left: Solo travel may seem a lonely pursuit, but you'll soon make friends

Opposite top right: A backpack and a camera are all a traveller needs

Opposite bottom right: The right time to book that big trip? Now

Of course...

There's more work to do before you head overseas on that grand solo adventure. Once you've taken the first step and booked in your trip, the rest is mere detail. Still, they're pretty important details. These are the little things you never thought of, and the big things you're not looking forward to tackling. But they're all completely necessary.

MAKE LISTS

Lists are your friend: big, long lists of all the things that need to be taken care of before you can get on that plane and not worry about anything back home at any point during your trip. Anytime you think of something to do, add it to the list. You can even write down things you've already done, and then cross them off straight away. It'll make you feel good.

GET INFORMED

Maybe you're going somewhere dangerous. Or maybe you're not. But the only way to know for sure is to get a good idea of what it's going to be like once you land. Check your government's travel advisory site – for instance, www.smartraveller. gov.au for Australians – but also check out travel forums and review websites to get advice from fellow travellers who might not be turned off by government warnings.

GET HEALTHY

The last thing you want on an extended journey to the middle of nowhere is to need to see a doctor. Before you leave it's worth not only going to your local GP for a general check-up, but also working on your fitness and tailoring it to your holiday. Going skiing? Climb some stairs. Going hiking? Get out and about on foot. And if you're a smoker, there's never been a better time to quit.

GET VACCINATED

After you've been to the GP, head to a specialist travel doctor and get vaccinated for the specific destinations you'll be visiting. Because nothing ruins your holiday quite like a bout of cholera.

PACK FOR YOUR DESTINATION

Don't just throw everything you own into a bag. And don't feel you need to stock up on expensive, travel-specific clothes, either. Take only the things you're comfortable wearing that will be suitable for your destination. Going to the Middle East? Take light clothes that will cover you up. Going to South-East Asia? Maybe leave the turtlenecks behind. Going to Northern Europe? Get ready to layer up, my friend. And bear in mind that if you've forgotten something important, you can probably buy it overseas. They have shops over there too, you know.

DON'T PACK TOO MUCH

It's tempting to take absolutely everything you own, but you really don't want to be carting that much around. Take enough underwear for about ten days, maximum. Take enough tops or shirts for the same amount of time. When you run out, do a load of washing. If you're going to need location-specific clothes like jackets a little later in your trip, plan to buy them once you've arrived. It'll save you from carrying around bulky things that you don't need for months on end.

PLAN TO BREAK UP YOUR TRIP WITH HOMESTAYS

When you're going on an extended trip – say, anything over a few months – the constant grind of hostels and dorm rooms will get to you after a while. On an epic journey you need to plan for some epic rest stops. Think you'll really like a certain city or destination? Book a week there in an apartment – say, through Airbnb. You'll be able to relax as if you were at home, cook your own food, and wash those disgusting clothes at last.

TIDY UP THE LOOSE ENDS

Before you leave, particularly for a long trip, there are plenty of annoying little things to take care of. You might be giving up your house or apartment, in which case you're going to have to sell your furniture, or organise somewhere to store it. You'll need to forward your mail on to someone as well – hopefully someone responsible. You'll also need to sort out how to pay any ongoing bills. Best thing to do is have them sent to you electronically so you can view and pay them on the go. Or, even better, cancel them all if you can.

DO THE BORING STUFF

This isn't fun. Still, before you leave you really need to take care of the travelling fine print: photocopy or scan your passport and travel documents and send copies to family and friends; organise your access to money overseas, including a travel card account and a way to get hold of emergency funds if you're robbed; give details, however vague, of your planned itinerary to parents or friends so someone always has a rough idea of where you are; and finally, get travel insurance. You'd be crazy to leave home without it.

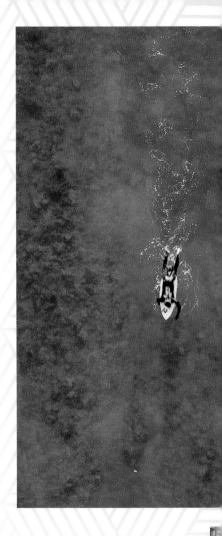

CHAPTER TWO

HOW TO STAY SAFE

Opposite top: The winding road to Forza d'Agro in Sicily, Italy

Opposite bottom left: Hong Kong buzzes with life

Opposite bottom right: Even a city like Sao Paulo, Brazil is manageable on your own

Top: The clear blue waters of the Maldives

The plane touches down in Dhaka and all hell breaks loose.

People are up and out of their seats as soon as the wheels have hit the ground, pulling bags down from lockers, dropping things on other passengers' heads, oblivious to the chaos they're causing. The air hostesses try in vain to keep everyone seated as boxes and plastic bags come crashing into the aisle.

This, as it turns out, is a pretty good introduction to Bangladesh.

I jump into a taxi. I need to get from the airport to the bus station to travel to the southern city of Chittagong. I've been to India, which borders Bangladesh, so I think I know what this will be like, that it will be a struggle to get there, just as it is to get anything done. Except I don't have a clue.

The traffic is insane, a dense knot of people and bicycles and carts and rickshaws and taxis and buses and trucks. The newer cars don't have the standard bumpers here but instead have big steel bars surrounding them in an attempt to protect pristine paintwork in a place that has no respect for pristine paintwork.

It's hot. My shirt is sticking to me in the back of the taxi. I stare, petrified and fascinated, through the front windscreen as cars and rickshaws and bikes dart across from every

direction. Horns honk. Touts yell. Strange smells waft in through the open window.

It's amazing how you can spend only a small amount of time in a country but it still leaves a permanent mark. Some destinations you'll barely be able to remember, despite having spent weeks there. But Bangladesh? Every detail of Bangladesh exists for me in technicolour. It's a wild place. Everything is a shock, like nothing I've ever seen or experienced before. It's all new, it's all different, it's all exciting. It's also kind of frightening.

The main bus station in the capital is actually just a small shed with an air conditioner that fights a losing battle against the dense heat. I buy a ticket and board a bus, watching in confusion as a man walks down the aisle, filming the passengers' faces with an old VHS camcorder that looks like it dropped in from 1980.

Soon our bus joins that knot of traffic outside and we make our way south along the scariest road I've ever been on in my entire life, a hellish stretch of constant near misses with every type of vehicle imaginable. I put on my headphones, close my eyes, pretend I'm in – I don't know – Baghdad. Anywhere but here.

It doesn't work. I'm forced to peek out every now and then at the chaos, as I feel the whoosh of another bus passing what feels like mere centimetres from our own. I can't help but look as we once again veer too close to the side of the road, sending pedestrians and livestock flying. And this goes on for hours. And hours.

It's pitch black when I'm finally dumped in Chittagong, at a featureless intersection of another busy street. I'm supposed to meet a friend, but she's not here. I might be in the wrong spot, I figure. Or maybe she forgot to come down.

This is a battle. I'm in a city I've never been before, where no one speaks my language, and I have nothing but an address scribbled on a piece of paper in my hand. I can't just front up to a hotel and stay there, because there are no hotels around here. Only market stalls and houses, rickshaws and chaos.

I find someone, eventually, who speaks English. He translates the address I've got on my piece of paper into the local language, finds me a cycle rickshaw and tells the guy where to go. I hop onto the metal seat, clutching my backpack, and hope things will be okay as we make very slow progress to the other side of town, through a city of four million people, which, it turns out, only has one set of traffic lights. And they don't work.

Over the next four days here, things will get interesting. I'll meet up with my friend, after spending hours trying to find her house. I'll hear tales from her and other expats of constant illness, and – not unrelated – of open sewers which always flood. I'll be laughed at because of my preference for shorts and flip-flops (only children wear shorts here, and only rickshaw drivers wear rubber flip-flops). I'll join an impromptu game of cricket that threatens to escalate into something more intimidating when groups of teenagers surround my friend, a Western girl in demure local dress, and we have to make a swift escape. I'll visit a museum dedicated to General Zia, the founder of Bangladeshi independence, housed in his former abode, which is still spattered with the murdered general's blood. And I will discover, thanks to my friend, the horrifying purpose of the video taken on that bus. The films are used, she'll tell me, to make it easier to identify the bodies in the highly likely event of an accident.

I'll take a night train back to Dhaka, instead of the dreaded bus. That train will crash. Seriously. The passengers will be marched off, put on buses, and sent back onto that road. I'll make it back to the airport, eventually, and I will bid this crazy country goodbye, having survived, having made it out safely – just. ●

There's no way to make travel completely safe.

Nor would you want it to be. A great journey will inevitably involve a few risks, a few leaps into the unknown. That trip I took to Bangladesh is permanently burned in my memory as one of the most eye-opening I've ever been on, one I'll be thinking and telling stories about for the rest of my life, but it certainly involved its share of risks. I didn't always feel safe there (and rightly so, as it turned out). Travel sometimes involves rolling the dice and dealing with whatever comes up, and that's all part of the fun.

There are, however, plenty of measures you can take to minimise those risks, to ensure you're equipped to deal with whatever the world throws at you on your big adventure. Solo travellers generally have to be more aware of their safety than people travelling in pairs or a group simply because you're more of a target when you're alone. Sad but true. It's natural that the scammers and touts and pickpockets of the world will aim for lone travellers, for those people with no support crew, which simply means you need to take more precautions.

This is particularly true, unfortunately, for female travellers.

Though in a perfect world women would be able to travel solo as freely as men, that's sadly not the case, and women going it alone will have to put more thought into their safety than their male colleagues. This doesn't mean you shouldn't go, or that you should be afraid to go. It simply means travelling with more concern for where you're going and who you can trust when you get there.

Many of the points in the following list apply to all travellers, but they're especially important for women who've decided to take the plunge and see the world on their own. You can pick up some extra tips by reading the fantastic blogs by solo female travellers out there, like those from Kiersten Rich (www.theblondeabroad.com), Dani Heinrich (www.globetrottergirls.com) and Liz Carlson (www.youngadventuress.com).

All travellers, however, should remember this one short caveat: don't be afraid. The world, on the whole, is a safe and welcoming place. Take these few precautions, and there's a very good chance that everything will be just fine.

SCAN YOUR PASSPORT AND EMAIL IT TO YOURSELF

Before setting off, scan the photo page of your passport, as well as your driver's licence and any other important documents, and email them to yourself, as well as to a close friend or relative. If you lose any of these documents, they'll be a whole lot easier to replace if you have the details handy.

TELL SOMEONE WHERE YOU'RE GOING. CHECK IN REGULARLY

This is a handy trick for solo travellers. Keep someone at home informed of your plans – share an itinerary before you leave, and also keep them up to date with any changes to where you're going and when you're likely to get there. Check in regularly to let them know that you're making it to these points safely.

TRY TO ARRIVE AT NEW DESTINATIONS DURING THE DAY

Though sometimes you won't have a choice, it's best not to arrive in a new city or country in the middle of the night, when you're forced to find your bearings under the cloak of darkness. Instead, time your transfers to get you to a new place around mid-afternoon, just in time for check-in.

WEAR OLD CLOTHES

Most solo travellers will instinctively realise that wearing chunky, obvious jewellery is a bad idea, but how about the rest of your outfit? It's tempting

Top: Public transport: an ideal way to get around

Bottom: The bright lights of London, UK

to look good when you're travelling; however, if you wear new, expensive clothes you're just going to draw attention to yourself. Instead, go for older gear in drab colours. Don't wear travel-specific clothing – branded hiking gear and the like – that will mark you out immediately as a visitor, but rather go with the everyday clothes you would wear at home. And if you need to carry expensive items like a camera or a laptop, do so in a tatty old bag that doesn't look as though it would be transporting anything valuable.

CARRY YOUR MONEY IN FRONT OF YOU; CARRY SMALL CHANGE

The chance of being the victim of petty crime in most countries is relatively low, but it still pays to be smart with your cash. Don't carry more than you'll need for the day; always put money in the front pocket of your jeans or trousers, rather than the back; and carry small change in a separate place to your larger bills, allowing you to pay for everyday items without pulling out a full wad for everyone to see.

DON'T STARE AT MAPS

In this age of smartphones equipped with various mapping apps, there's really no need to carry a hard-copy map and mark yourself out as a tourist by stopping to check it in public places. Instead, just check your phone; or, if you don't want to show off that piece

of expensive gadgetry, sit down at a cafe and grab a drink before taking out your map or guidebook to peruse.

DON'T USE A MONEY BELT

This is my golden rule of safe travel. Money belts – the thin, bum-bag-like satchels that travellers are supposed to use to 'hide' their cash and important documents – are very easy for an experienced thief to spot bulging from below your waistband. If anything, these belts just show people you have something to steal. Better to simply leave anything important at the hostel, or at home.

TRUST YOUR INSTINCTS

You will be approached a lot, as a solo traveller. You will be approached by touts and swindlers, by con artists and others with nefarious intent; however, those people will be in the extreme minority. You will also be approached on your journey by a huge number of locals and other travellers who have nothing but goodwill and a generous spirit. Often the trick to spotting the difference between these two types is experience – knowledge of the local scams, of the classic tricks – but it's also worth listening to your gut. If a situation feels wrong to you, if you're getting a bad feeling about the person you're with or the place that you're in, then get out. It's far better to be on the safe side here.

DON'T MAKE EYE CONTACT

It saddens me to have to write this, because I believe in interacting with as many locals as possible when you travel, and being as open and as interested as you can be. However, if you're in a place where you're being approached a lot, where you're constantly having to make that call between safe and potentially dangerous, it can be a lot easier to just keep your head down and not allow people that initial 'in' by making eye contact with you.

ASK AROUND ABOUT CLASSIC SCAMS

In most cities there will be a standard set of scams that tourists fall for on an almost daily basis. 'I just want to practise my English.' 'Would you like to see my cousin's jewellery store?' 'I'm an art student ...' And so on. Ask someone at your hostel for the local classics to watch out for.

DON'T GET TOO DRUNK

You lose your inhibitions when you're drunk. You also make terrible decisions. If you're travelling by yourself, go out for a few drinks, by all means, but try not to let it get out of hand.

GET A GROUP TOGETHER TO GO OUT AT NIGHT

In some cities it will be perfectly safe for you to go out at night on your own. That's great, it's part of the adventure. It's worth asking the staff at your hostel, though, if they think it's a good idea. If not, try to gather a group of like-minded souls from around the dorm rooms to join you on your night out. Failing that, many hostels organise nightly outings in cities where it may not seem safe to go solo.

GET SOMEONE TO CALL YOU A TAXI, OR USE UBER

Leaving a bar or restaurant or hotel late at night? Rather than flagging down a random taxi from the street, have someone from that bar or restaurant or hotel call you a taxi. This ensures the job has been logged into a system and the driver is someone accountable and legit. Alternatively, if Uber is operating in the city you're visiting, it might be safer and more reliable than the local taxi service.

GET INSURANCE

This is crucial. Don't leave home without buying travel insurance. You can take all of the precautions in the world, but you can't plan for bad luck. Insurance will cover you, and get you out of some serious jams.

CHAPTER THREE

HOW TO SURVIVE ON YOUR OWN

Opposite top left: The luggage dilemma in Florence, Italy

Opposite top right: Reflecting on life in Singapore

Opposite bottom: Go your own way in the Atacama Desert, Chile

Bottom: The charming streets of George Town, Malaysia

Personal safety will not end up being your main concern.

You might be thinking, right now, about all of the bad things that can happen while you travel the world solo, the potential muggings and swindles and other sticky situations, but really, those are remote possibilities. The problems you're most likely to face on your travels are the small ones, the awkward ones, the logistical head-scratchers that take a little time to figure out.

Things just aren't as simple when you're travelling on your own. Suddenly, eating out at a restaurant feels kind of weird. Going for a swim at the beach is problematic. Even going to the toilet at an airport or a bus station is a drama.

Fortunately, there are ways to deal with all of these issues.

Top: Tuk-tuks are cheap, and they're also an adventure

Bottom: Solo travel means time to yourself

HOW DO I EAT OUT AT RESTAURANTS ALONE

Admittedly, it feels strange to begin with, and it will for a while. There's no trick to eating out at a restaurant on your own – it's just something you have to get used to. To ease yourself in, try to stick to more casual restaurants, cafes, pubs or bars, places with a high turnover of patrons and a relaxed, easygoing atmosphere. At fancy restaurants you'll feel a lot more out of place on a table for one.

Take a book to read while you wait for your food. Use your phone or an iPad to log on to the free wifi – which many casual eateries now offer – and read the news, or update your social media. Take out your diary and write some notes. These are all pleasant distractions, though the truth is that they're not really necessary, and soon you'll feel comfortable just sitting there and taking everything in.

HOW DO I DRINK AT BARS ALONE

Bars work in reverse to restaurants: embrace the fancy joints, leave the casual places until you've made a few friends. While you may feel out of place nursing a beer on your own in a rowdy pub, at a classy cocktail or speakeasy-style bar it's far easier to grab a stool, chat to the bartender, order a nice drink, and then nurse it for a few hours while you watch the night unfold. Pairing your drinking with dining – say, at a tapas bar – might also ease any social anxiety.

HOW DO I SLEEP WELL IN A DORM

Sharing your bedroom with five or six strangers can be a daunting prospect. Dorm-room accommodation in hostels is definitely the cheapest way to travel, but it's not always the easiest. Where do you store your bags? How do you get a good night's sleep? What if you hate everyone in your room?

Dorms really aren't that bad, though. Most hostels – in particular, the ones recommended in this book – offer secure storage for your backpack and other valuables. If you're a light sleeper, always pack earplugs and an eye mask. And relax about the company. You won't get on with everyone, but the majority of travellers are laidback, friendly types who are easy to get to know.

HOW DO I CARRY MY BAGS

Here's the trick: don't pack more than you can carry. You generally need far less on the road than you think, and if carrying your bag at home is a nightmare, then lugging it around foreign cities is going to be about a hundred times worse. So take the clothes and accessories and gadgets you think you'll need, and halve them: your life just became a whole lot easier. Another option to consider is buying a bag with wheels. If you're only going to be travelling in big cities, or sticking mostly to the Western world, it's unlikely you'll require the rough-terrain freedom that a backpack provides. Make life easy for yourself.

HOW DO I NAVIGATE

You might not be able to read a map, but you can definitely read Google Maps. Just follow the blue line. Free wifi is available in pretty much every hostel around the world, as well as in plenty of cafes, bars and restaurants, meaning you'll always be able to access your phone's features and use them to help you get around a city – including catching Ubers and figuring out the public transport system – for free.

HOW DO I GO SWIMMING

Here's the problem for solo travellers: you're at the beach and you want to swim, but who's going to look after your stuff? Who's going to watch all your valuables while you're in the water? There's no easy way around this, aside from just not taking anything valuable. If you know you're heading for the beach, pack only your swimming gear, your room key and a small amount of cash. Place your gear as close to the water as possible while you go for a splash, so you can keep an eye on it. That way a robbery is unlikely, and you won't lose anything of value if it does happen.

HOW DO I GO TO THE TOILET

'Watch my bags, I'll be right back.' You don't realise the beauty of that sentence until you have no one to say it to. What do you do when you're in an airport or a train station or a bus station and you're desperate to go to the toilet, but you're stuck with a huge backpack and armfuls of souvenirs? Unfortunately, the answer is you take it all into the toilet cubicle with you. Just cram it all in. If you're somewhere like Japan, you can usually leave your backpack safely in the main bathroom area – anywhere else, however, and it's all coming in. If you really don't want to, though, a lot of stations have left-luggage facilities where you can pay a small amount to store your gear (also handy if you plan to head into town for the day).

HOW DO I TAKE PHOTOS WITH ME IN THEM

You'll have plenty of time to take photos when you're travelling alone. Unfortunately, either you won't be in them, or your face will be taking up the entire frame (at the expense of all that beautiful landscape). To nail a really great shot of yourself in situ, you have two options: polish your selfie game by investing in an otherwise annoying selfie stick or rely on the kindness of strangers. Pick the person with the biggest camera (who clearly knows what they're doing), and ask them to grab a shot of you.

HOW DO I EXPLAIN THAT I'M ALONE

There's a social stigma in some countries, particularly for women, attached to being alone. Where's your husband? Why aren't you married yet? Aren't you scared? Sometimes, admitting you're alone can make you feel vulnerable, or embarrassed, and

There's a difference between being alone and being lonely. The two don't necessarily go together.

these are totally legitimate concerns. There are ways to deal with this. If you're feeling really uncomfortable, you can wear a fake wedding ring, and explain that your partner is doing something different today. You can also avoid awkward questions by asking a few of your own. If you'd prefer to go for the honest approach, then declare you're flying solo with pride. This is an amazing thing you're doing – people should hear about it.

HOW DO I MAKE FRIENDS

This is another of those skills that may not come easy at first, but will be second nature after a long period of travelling alone. For the full run-down on how to meet people in foreign lands, flip to chapter five (*see* p. 44) of this book.

WHAT IF I GET LONELY

There's a difference between being alone and being lonely. The two don't necessarily go together. There will be times when homesickness really strikes, when the feeling of freedom that solo travel engenders is obscured, briefly, by a longing for company. And that's fine. The way to deal with it is to throw yourself into social situations, to sign up for a group outing at your hostel, to book a day tour, to do something fun that will remind you of why you decided to do this in the first place, and why your friends back home are so jealous that you did.

WHAT IF I GET SICK

Getting sick when you have someone to care for you is no fun; getting sick when you're on your own is worse. This is something you may have to battle through on your own, which will be character building, if nothing else. To try to avoid this situation, make sure all of your vaccinations are up to date, and follow basic food safety rules when you're travelling (i.e. cook it, boil it, peel it or forget it). If you are feeling ill, try to get to a local doctor or medical clinic for a quick check-up to make sure it's nothing too serious. Once you're feeling better, treat yourself to a nice meal or some sort of fun experience to toast your recovery in style.

CHAPTER FOUR

HOW TO MAKE IT AFFORDABLE

Opposite top: Buses are one of the cheapest forms of public transport

Opposite middle: Street food: your ticket to a tasty, affordable meal

Opposite bottom: Dorm rooms will soon become your friend

Bottom: Travel like a local to save cash

'What are we getting for lunch?'

I yelled in Khien's ear as we roared through Dong Mang, a small town on the road to Dalat.

'Chicken!' he yelled from the front of the motorbike, dodging a car and narrowly missing a stray dog. 'We will cook it later!'

Okay, I thought, chicken. Of all the things I'd eaten in Vietnam, this would be up there with the least adventurous. It was no snake or fried insect, but it sounded good. So the two of us motored towards the central market, darting through the usual melange of honking scooters and trucks and pedestrians and livestock that fills a typical Vietnamese road.

The market was the sort you'd find in almost every town here, with tarpaulin sheets rigged over a concrete floor, large stacks of fresh fruit and vegetables, and herbs laid out on wooden benches. Khien wasn't there for herbs, though: he headed straight to the back to find his chicken lady. I just tried to keep up.

Even in a country that's already cheap, this is how you make travel more affordable. You don't go to restaurants three times a day – you do what the locals do, and shop in markets. You buy what the locals buy. You cook what the locals cook. And what they cook is always a snapshot of their culture, unadulterated and real. Whether that's cheese in Paris or mystery meat on a stick in Tanzania, salumi in Bologna or weird nutty things in Moscow, market produce is endlessly interesting, and endlessly affordable. It's win-win.

Dong Mang, of course, is cheap. It's *so* cheap. I was travelling through Vietnam on a budget, choosing to see the country alone (a few years after that first encounter with Son in Hanoi). I'd booked a stripped-back motorbike tour from Nha Trang to Dalat, and was sleeping on the floor in traditional homes, clinging to the back of an old bike as we cruised along winding, potholed roads, eating simple meals made with produce bought from the markets and cooked in the way everyone else in this part of the world cooked them.

So Khien, my guide, and I pushed through the busy market, with me smiling into the many staring faces of the vendors there, politely declining to buy the huge bags of things that were proffered, trying to keep up with Khien as he ducked and weaved through the crowd. We arrived at a small stand at the back of the market, where the realisation finally dawned.

We weren't here to buy chicken – we were here to buy *a* chicken. And when you buy a chicken at a Vietnamese market, it tends to look more animated than the ones in the freezer section at your local supermarket back home. These chickens were proper chickens. Clucking, pecking chickens. Living chickens.

'Which one do you like?' Khien asked, pointing at the ten chooks nervously pacing around a little enclosure.

I wasn't totally comfortable with this situation – I'd never chosen my lunch live before – but what could I do? I didn't want Khien to think I was ... well, chicken, so I surveyed the pen of potential sustenance. Having never chosen meat of such freshness, I wasn't sure what to look for. They all looked scrawny and feathery to me.

'What about that scrawny, feathery one?' I said to Khien.

'Okay.' He nodded. 'We get that one.'

You see some fantastically strange things in local markets. There's a stall in Phonsavanh, Laos, that sells bats. Not single bats, but bats tied together in little bundles of three. Because why would you want only one or two bats? Go to Tsukiji fish market in Tokyo and you'll find seafood you didn't even know existed, the sort of things that should be wobbling through horror movie sets, not presenting themselves on your dinner plate.

You also see reality in a local market, cold and hard. You see where food really comes from. And I was about to see the origins of mine.

Khien and I watched as the lady did what needed to be done to our scrawny little chicken, working so swiftly that within a few minutes she presented us with a simple plucked carcass, the sort you'd find in the freezer section of your local supermarket back home.

Lunch. Into a plastic bag, into Khien's backpack, and then off on the motorbike to a clearing in a forest where we'd be able to start a fire and cook up our prize. Organic and fresh. Free range, I assumed. And it only set us back US$2. ●

How much is this adventure going to cost?

That's a question you have to ask anytime you plan a trip away, but it's even more important when you're travelling solo. Costs can balloon when you don't have anyone to share a hotel room or meals, when you have to catch taxis and book tours and see the sights alone. This is one of the few obvious downsides to solo travel: the fact that everything just seems to cost more.

Still, it's manageable. There are tricks to keeping your expenditure as low as possible, to ensure this whole thing is viable. You simply have to be smart; you have to think about what you're spending, and how you could reduce it or avoid it altogether.

Most of the hacks for doing that are not a big deal, and they won't impact heavily on your travel experience. In fact, some of these ideas will actually improve your trip immensely – they'll force you to have new and amazing experiences, to mix with people you may not otherwise have mixed with. My trip to the markets in central Vietnam was a perfect example. Sure, it was rough, and eye-opening, but it was also extremely cheap and pleasingly authentic, a true slice of local Vietnamese life. There's no way a meal in a sterile, air-conditioned restaurant could compare to that in any respect.

The money-saving tips that follow will become second nature after a while on the road. You'll barely even remember that you're scrimping. All you'll think about is the fact you now have the freedom to explore the world on your own, without having to pay more than everyone else for the privilege.

Top left: The ultimate road trip in Moab, USA

Top right: Street food culture in Hanoi, Vietnam

Middle left: Paris's famed Arc de Triomphe

Bottom left: Locals pose for a selfie in Kyoto, Japan

19 ways to make solo travel more affordable.

The tips and tricks that will help you get the most out of your journey while keeping costs to a minimum.

BE FLEXIBLE WHEN CHOOSING YOUR DESTINATION

The great thing about travelling solo is the freedom to be flexible, to change your plans at the last minute and not have to run that decision by anyone. This freedom can also help you save money. If you're prepared to scan the internet for cheap flights or good deals, and jump on a plane at any time and go anywhere, you'll save huge amounts of money.

PACK LIGHT

Here's an easy way to save a few hundred dollars: pack light enough to only require hand luggage when you fly. That way you'll avoid checked baggage fees on shorter domestic flights, and any journey with a budget carrier. It might mean wearing the same clothes a few times before you get the chance to wash them – but, hey, you're travelling on your own. Who cares?

TRAVEL IN OFF-PEAK PERIODS

Rome in January is spectacular. The skies are blue, the air is crisp but not cold, the locals are relaxed and happy, and there are almost no tourists around. It's perfect. It's also the perfect example of the joy of travelling in off-peak periods: not only will you save money, as hostels offer specials and attractions reduce their prices, but you'll be able to avoid the bulk of the crowds in super-touristy locations. Even shoulder seasons, the likes of autumn and spring, will allow you to save money but still see a destination close to its best.

BOOK TOURS WITH NO SINGLE SUPPLEMENT

As long as you're prepared to share a room with a stranger, you can book a spot with most tour companies for the same price it will cost someone travelling as a twosome. Intrepid, G Adventures and On The Go are specialists for this sort of travel. If you're not keen to share, though, there are a few companies, such as Single Travel Connections and Two's A Crowd, that don't charge a single supplement for people who want their own room.

MANAGE YOUR MONEY

This is important for all travellers, but especially those going it alone. You want to make sure you can access your money and spend as little as possible for the privilege. That means looking into credit cards that don't charge foreign transaction fees, or ATM fees. It means checking out specialised travel cards that allow you to load up with various foreign currencies and take advantage of good exchange rates. It also means you can plan ahead so you don't need to make cash currency exchanges in airports, where you'll always get ripped off.

BE SMART WITH YOUR PHONE

Most travellers will take a mobile phone overseas with them – but you don't want to be hit with a massive bill. In this regard, free wifi is your friend. Pretty much every hostel in the world offers free wifi, and plenty of cafes and bars do too. To save money, ensure your global data roaming is switched off, and instead use wifi for all of your email, WhatsApp, Skype, social media and general surfing needs. If you're going to be in a country longer than a couple of weeks, it's also worth looking into purchasing a local SIM. These pre-paid cards are usually far cheaper than roaming that uses your SIM from home. If you're only staying a short time, just try to keep phone calls and messages to a minimum, and use free wifi for everything else.

USE RAIL PASSES OR OTHER DISCOUNT TRANSPORT CARDS

In most cities and countries that are considered expensive for backpackers, you'll be able to buy discount travel cards aimed at visitors. In Japan, the JR Pass provides huge savings if you're planning to use intercity trains. In Barcelona, the Hola BCN card will score you unlimited rides on the city's public transport system. And the Stockholm Travelcard allows unlimited access to all public transport in the city for a set period of time at a discounted rate. These are just a few examples from around the world – it's certainly worth googling the destinations you've chosen to see if they offer something similar.

STAY IN HOSTELS

Hostels are ideal for solo travellers. They usually offer extremely cheap accommodation, in shared dorm rooms, and their kitchen facilities allow you to cook your own food. Plus, they provide social environments in which to meet fellow travellers with whom you can band together to save money on things like transport and attractions.

USE THE SHARING ECONOMY

There is, of course, an even cheaper accommodation option than a hostel bed, and that's couch surfing: staying for free with locals who offer up their spare beds, or couches, or living room floors for travellers to sleep on. If you're not comfortable with that model, you can rent a room in someone's house through Airbnb. To use the sharing economy when it comes to transport, meanwhile, look into UberPool (where you can share Uber rides with others), or BlaBlaCar, which puts travellers in touch with others heading in the same direction.

FILL UP ON BREAD

There's a classic mantra at any all-you-can-eat buffet: don't fill up on bread. This doesn't hold true for solo travellers at a hostel or hotel breakfast. If you're staying somewhere that offers a free meal to start the day, fill up on bread. That is, fill your pockets with bread rolls and croissants. Roll up some ham and cheese in a napkin. Put a couple of pieces of fruit in a bag. Boom: you don't have to pay for lunch.

USE PUBLIC TRANSPORT

This is such a simple money-saver. Forgo taxis and tourist mini-vans and even Ubers and get around town the cheaper way. Catch public buses. Ride the subway. Alternatively, opt for ultra-cheap forms of private transport, like rickshaws or tuk-tuks or motorbike taxis. You'll not only get where you're going, but you'll also meet interesting people, experience local life and walk away with a story to tell.

JOIN FREE TOURS

Most major cities around the world now offer at least one or two options to take a guided tour for absolutely no cost. These are usually walking tours hosted by passionate locals who'll show you the sights and talk you through the quirks of their culture, at no charge. Beats an open-top bus tour any day of the week.

GO TO FREE ATTRACTIONS

Some of the world's best tourist attractions cost absolutely nothing to experience. Pretty much all of the major museums and art galleries in London, for example, are free to enter. Central Park in New York is free. The Smithsonian in Washington, DC, is free. The Grand Bazaar in Istanbul is free. And viewing street art in any city will cost you nothing.

DO THE ACTIVITIES ORGANISED BY YOUR HOSTEL

Here's another reason to stay at a hostel: most places organise activities and tours of their local area, including pub crawls, walking tours, nightclub visits and more, which offer far more value than if you attempted to go out by yourself. You'll also meet plenty of people to share future costs with.

SHOP IN MARKETS; COOK YOUR OWN FOOD

Though eating local food is a huge part of the travel experience, you can save a lot of money by buying fresh produce and cooking it yourself in the hostel kitchen. And if you choose to shop at local markets, rather than generic supermarkets, you'll still be able to tap in to the true cuisine of the country. You'll also be supporting the local economy, as your money goes straight into the hands of the farmers and growers. If you really can't be bothered cooking and still want to save, street food – particularly in South-East Asia – is an inexpensive way of eating great local cuisine.

DRINK AT HAPPY HOUR

Hostel bars always offer happy-hour discounts, and it's no coincidence that they're usually packed around these times: backpackers love a drinks special. But you don't have to stick to the hostel. If you're in any area that's popular with budget travellers, you'll find most of the local bars and restaurants will do discounted drinks at certain times of the day. In Europe, your ticket to affordable boozing is the supermarket, where you'll find local beer and wine that's an absolute steal.

PAIR UP

Jealous of all those travelling twosomes and other groups saving money by sharing cabs and meals and the like? Then copy them. Get together with like-minded solo travellers – people you meet in hostels, on tours, and in myriad other ways – and hit the road. You'll save money travelling together, and you can always go your separate ways if things don't work out.

WALK

Here's an even cheaper way to get around town: walk. Use two feet and a heartbeat and you will be forced to slow down, to take everything in properly, to see and feel and touch and smell the city around you. And it will be absolutely free.

EAT LUNCH OUT, AND DINNER IN

If you're keen to eat out a few times in nice restaurants but you don't think you can afford it, then lunchtime dining is for you. In Europe, plenty of restaurants do set-menu lunches (two or three courses and a glass of wine) at a far cheaper price than you'd pay at the same establishment in the evening. In Japan, many of the fancier restaurants drop their prices significantly at lunchtime. Eat lunch out, and cook dinner at the hostel, and you've saved yourself a packet.

Top: Walking: the cheapest, and often best, form of transport

Bottom: Lunch at a ramen bar in Tokyo, Japan

Opposite top: There's always a chance to meet people in a hostel

Opposite bottom: Tourists pose at Fushimi Inari Shrine in Kyoto, Japan

Top: One of the crowd in Miami, USA

Bottom: Hit the beach in Mar del Plata, Argentina

CHAPTER FIVE

HOW TO MEET PEOPLE

'You just never know who you'll sit next to,' says Frank, smiling, his west coast Kiwi accent as strong as ever.

He takes another bite of his roast lamb, stares into the distance.

He's right, I realise. You never know who you'll sit next to. Frank and his friends hadn't seemed too remarkable an hour ago, when I'd joined them for dinner and they'd introduced themselves as 'a bunch of broken-down old skiers'. But as pre-meal drinks morph into entrees, and entrees into mains, they let slip enough to prove that they are more than that – much more.

These broken-down old skiers are from a club ski field near Christchurch. They've made the short road journey to Ohau in search of more of the white stuff, and a few drops of the red stuff. It's a tiny ski resort, Ohau, barely bigger than Frank's club field. At Ohau, when they say 'all lifts are open', they mean both of them. It's the kind of place where if you accidentally crash into someone in the morning, you'll invariably end up beside them on the double-chair ski lift in the afternoon.

Everyone seems to know everyone, and that's not simply because they're locals who've been carving these runs their whole lives. Some of the friends chatting on the piste got to know each other only the night before, while they were on the, um, piste. They're probably staying where I'm staying, at Lake Ohau Lodge, the small hotel owned by the Neilson family, who also own the ski hill and the canteen, and just about everything else around here.

The lodge is a classic of the ski-field scene. There's a large common room in the middle, the kind of place you can picture snow lovers wearing ridiculous knitted jumpers standing around a log fire, trading war stories from a day on the slopes. You can picture this because it's happening right now.

While breakfast here is a staggered affair – like the guests, who lurch in at different times to fuel up for the day ahead – dinner is a formal group event. The kids eat first at a table all their own, and then the adults are seated according to a plan that exists solely in owner Jock Neilson's head. I sit there in my silly jumper, drinking a Speight's ale by the fire until Jock fronts up: 'Okay, are you ready to sit down?' Then I'm placed at a table with complete strangers – and you never know who you'll sit next to.

Everyone has a story, you just have to tease it out of them. First night I'm sitting with a guy called Mike, who lets slip that he flies planes. For a living? Yeah, Mike flies planes for a living. What sort of planes? Hercules planes, he says. Mike flies Hercules planes for a living.

That sounds like something you'd do in the Air Force, someone says. Well, yeah, Mike admits, he *is* in the Air Force. Mike flies Hercules planes in the Air Force for a living.

Been anywhere dangerous? Well, Mike says, he just got back from one of several stints he's had in Afghanistan. So there you have it: Mike, the Brisbane dad who's learning to ski, also flies Hercules planes in Afghanistan for a living. Interesting guy.

On night number two, Jock summons me from a fireside reverie to sit on a table with a bunch of ageing Kiwis, the broken-down old skiers. Frank is the first to crack: he's a priest, he says, who has spent the bulk of his life spreading the good word through Brazil.

He's also a mountaineer. Turns out he and his mate Keith from across the table used to do some serious climbing together – they worked as alpine guides on Mount Cook, and one year spent 100 days having a crack at Mount Everest, but fell agonisingly short.

Keith sips at his glass of wine, then reveals that he didn't always work on Mount Cook; he did a bit 'down south', too. Down south, I say. Invercargill? He grins. Antarctica.

Keith used to do a bit of work in Antarctica. Right. What sort of work? He was in search-and-rescue, he says, based at McMurdo Station. Ever have any big missions? Well, yeah, Keith admits. He was first on the scene when an Air New Zealand plane carrying 257 people crashed into Mount Erebus in 1979. He led the recovery.

Keith led the recovery of the Air New Zealand disaster in Antarctica. You want stories? The guy has hundreds of them.

And this, I'm thinking, while Keith launches into yet another tale, is what solo travel is all about: the people. The fascinating people you'd never normally meet.

Doesn't matter if you're at a dining table at Ohau or on a bus in Moscow or at a bar in Lima. You just never know who you'll sit next to. •

This will be the highlight of your journey.

It doesn't matter where you're going, or how long you're going for. It doesn't matter what you'll see, or the things you'll do. The truly memorable part of your time away from home – the part you'll carry with you for the rest of your life – will be the people you meet along the way.

Fellow travellers. Locals. New friends. New partners. New travel buddies. New contacts. Funny people. Amazing people. Interesting people. Annoying people. Beautiful people. You'll discover them all and so many more on this grand solo journey. And there's no need to worry: even if you're not good at meeting people, you will still meet them. This isn't a 'maybe' proposition. People will just come at you when you travel; they will appear from a million different places, sometimes the least expected.

They will sleep in your dorm room and they will cook dinner in your kitchen. They will sign up for the same tour and they will drink in the same bar. They will just happen to get on the same bus as you or begin their journey at the same time.

These are people who are sharing the very same experiences, who can relate to the highs and lows, who understand the beauty and the difficulty of travelling alone. And they'll probably be keen to meet new friends too – to hear your story and tell their own. They might be looking for someone to share a journey with; they might just be looking for someone to share a beer. If you want to meet people while you're away, you most definitely will. And there are a few sure-fire places to find them.

AT YOUR HOSTEL

Stay at a hostel, and you will meet people. Hundreds of people. It will start in your room, if it's a dorm, which will almost certainly be filled with fellow solo travellers, or groups of friends. Dorms not only help you save money, but force you to meet people. They throw you together in a small space with travellers you can't help but make conversation with. You'll meet people from all around the world in a hostel dorm room, from Europe and the Americas, from Asia and Australia. All you have to do is sit on your bunk and wait for them to walk through the door. Ask where they're from, and where they just came from, and you're away.

Hostels have other shared spaces, too, which are ideal for meeting those who may not have wound up in the same dorm as you. In the kitchens you'll have plenty of time to stand around and chat while your dodgy spaghetti bolognese comes together. In the lounge areas you'll be able to swap tips with those who've already been to the places you plan to visit. And by joining group activities organised by your hostel – weekly barbecues or pub crawls or walking tours of the local area – you'll have even more chances to chat to new people.

ON A DAY TOUR

So you've rocked up in a new city and you don't know any of the attractions, or any people. No problem. Your answer is a day tour, a short snapshot of this destination, provided by a local, in the company of fellow travellers. Ones like walking tours of the Marais in Paris; street-food tours in Mexico City; craft brewery tours in Portland. Some are run by local companies and operators that you'll be able to find through your hostel, while others are run by larger, global companies such as Urban Adventures and Airbnb. Whatever you choose, you'll gain an insight into this new place you've just arrived in, plus spend the day with other travellers who might very quickly become new friends.

ON A LONGER TOUR

Rather than doing a day tour, why not spend longer with a group? Let someone else – your tour guide and driver – do all of the hard work for a few days, a few weeks, or even a few months. Join a tour and you'll not only hit all of the hotspots in your chosen destination, but you'll be thrown together with a bunch of like-minded travellers with whom to share the experience.

AT A CLASS

You don't have to commit to a tour in order to meet people. Just a few hours at a class will throw you into the company of potential new friends. Take a cooking class while you're overseas – learn a few recipes, meet fellow travellers. Enrol in a language course, which will introduce you to plenty of classmates, and also help you communicate with locals. Learn to dance. Learn to paint or draw. Even if the people you share the class with don't turn out to be your type, you'll walk away with a new appreciation of a local passion.

AT WORK

Plenty of backpackers work overseas as a way to supplement their savings and keep the dream alive. The real bonus of a job, though, is the people you meet while working. Teach English at a school. Get work behind a bar. Wait tables at a cafe. Clean rooms to pay for your board at a hostel. There are also plenty of volunteering opportunities out there, including WWOOFing (Worldwide Opportunities on Organic Farms – i.e. doing volunteer farm work), and other social enterprises. Do good, make friends. Easy.

AT A BAR

Of course, you don't have to be working at a bar to meet people. You can just go in on your own. While it's a little intimidating heading out solo, bars and pubs in backpacker-friendly districts are social areas where most people are up for a chat. If you're feeling confident, simply head out to a bar, grab yourself a drink and a seat, let that delightful foreign accent of yours rip, and wait for new friends to arrive.

AT A SOCIAL MEDIA MEET-UP

Even if you're not staying at a hostel or doing a tour, you can meet fellow travellers at 'meet-ups' organised through various web-based media. The website Meetup, unsurprisingly, organises regular meet-ups in cities around the world for travellers, and those keen to meet travellers. 'InstaMeets' are organised through Instagram. Various traveller meets are also held by the Twitter community (check out #meetup to get started). Get online, and get socialising.

ON TINDER

Don't laugh: this is for real. Even if you're not looking for a hook-up. Even if you just want to hang out with a local or a fellow traveller for a night. If you want to go out for dinner, or go out to a bar, Tinder can be the answer. Get on there and get swiping, and remember to be honest about your intentions and your limits.

Opposite left: Try a group tour to hook up with fellow travellers

Opposite top right: Cafes and bars are perfect places to meet locals

Opposite bottom right: New friends: they're out there waiting for you

Get online, and get socialising.

The 8 worst types of people to travel with.

You're going to meet hundreds of people when you travel. Some of these interactions will be fleeting affairs, while others may go on for years. Travellers naturally tend to band together, to join forces and hit the road in groups, for added safety, affordability, enjoyment.

And that's a truly great thing. You should share this experience with other people, with people from different cultures, different countries. Fun people. Crazy people. But not everyone makes a great travel partner. After you've been on the road for a while, once you've spent time with various people and observed their habits, you'll find there are certain types that make amazing travel buddies, and certain types that really don't. If you spot any of the following traits in your potential partners, bid them farewell ...

THE TIGHTWAD

'Twenty bucks? Yeah, I dunno.' You get a sinking feeling the first time you hear a sentence like that, when you realise your travel partner has short arms and long pockets. Different travellers have different budgets, sure – but there are also people who just seem allergic to spending money. When you're travelling together, that's kind of a nightmare. The flipside, of course, is the rampant spender, who can also be annoying if you don't have as much money to shell out. Ideally, you'll find a travel buddy who has a similar budget to yours, and a similar willingness to dip into it.

THE DRUNK

There's nothing wrong with a drink. Travellers drink all the time. It's fun. But there is a big difference between a drinker and a drunk. Drinkers use booze as a sweetener to an already great experience; for drunks, the booze is the experience. Travelling with someone who's constantly on the lookout for the next bar, who gets smashed and makes an arse of themselves and needs to be carried home every night, gets pretty old pretty quickly.

THE FAFFER

You watch the Faffer getting ready in the morning, and you gauge how long it'll be before they'll be set to go. Okay, you think, they need to put their shoes on, to pack a few things in their bag – should be out the door in ten minutes. And yet, half an hour later, you're still there sitting on the bed while the Faffer ambles about the room, picking things up and putting them down again, remembering things they've forgotten, deciding to change their outfit, reconsidering the day's plans ... Argh! Let's just go!

THE STRESSHEAD

Stress is contagious. If the person you're travelling with is stressing, then you'll start stressing. You'll stress over the thing they're stressing over, and you'll also stress over the fact that the other person is stressing again. They'll see that and start stressing even more. It's a vicious circle. The ultimate travel buddy will be able to roll with the punches, will not worry too much about missed trains or bad accommodation, or about any of the little problems that travel inevitably entails. Stressheads just make those things worse.

THE FUSSY EATER

I have no problem with people who want to be vegan or vegetarian or pescatarian, or carnivore or omnivore or even fruitarian – everyone is entitled to follow the diet that's best for them. When it becomes a problem is when you travel with someone whose diet is very restricted. Food is a huge part of your travel experience. It's something to love and something to share. When you're travelling with someone whose diet is completely different from yours, especially a diet that needs to be specifically catered for in a country that may not be very good at catering for it, food can become a huge problem.

THE PRINCESS/PRINCE

You have to be adventurous when you travel. You have to open yourself up to life the way locals experience it. That might mean eating in restaurants that look dirty, or sleeping on floors, or walking long distances, or doing any one of a million things that might take you out of your comfort zone. Anyone who isn't open to a little discomfort is not going to be fun to travel with.

THE WAVERER

Travel involves decisions – a lot of decisions. Where should we go today? What should we eat? Where should we drink? How should we get there? Where should we go next? How much should we pay for a hotel? Which hotel should it be? And on, and on, and on. If you're travelling with someone who has trouble making decisions, who constantly swings from one side to the other, who lives in fear of making the wrong call, it will be a *looooong* trip.

THE WHINGER

This is the worst. You can deal with almost any other type of traveller. You can put up with drunks, with faffers, with stressheads, with tightwads and vegans galore. But whingers are a nightmare. Whingers seem determined to have a bad time when they travel, no matter where they go. They seem to be able to fixate on the one thing that might have gone wrong and make a big deal out of it. A good travel experience is all about having the right attitude, and whingers definitely do not have it. Make sure you travel with people who want to have a good time.

CHAPTER SIX

HOW TO GET AROUND

Opposite top right: A lonely highway in the Namib Desert, Namibia

Opposite bottom left: A boat putters between islands off the west coast of Thailand, near Khao Lak

Opposite bottom right: Cars aren't cheap - but they do provide plenty of freedom

Top: Bright lights in Berlin, Germany

The stares are a dead giveaway.

Not many Westerners get on this bus. Probably with good reason, too. Seven or eight sets of eyes widen and lock on to me as I lug my bag up the grimy stairs and start looking for a place to perch for the next few hours. There are plenty of spare seats: velour-covered benches of varying colours.

'Sit!' the driver yells. 'Anywhere!' He's yelling to make himself heard above the Bollywood music booming from the dodgy old stereo balanced on top of his dashboard. It's a big bus with not many people on board, so I sling my pack onto the sticky fabric, take the seat next to it and settle in among the staring passengers and the smell of motor oil and the sound of Bollywood glamour.

It's hard to know how long I'll be sitting here. Officially, the journey from Chennai to Mamallapuram takes three hours, but time is elastic in this place, dependent upon traffic and mechanics and the whims of the thousands of gods who are in charge around here. One of those gods, Ganesh, sits on the dash next to the stereo, so we can assume he's on our side. There's a crack in the windscreen in front of him, but no one seems concerned. It's also about 40°C (104°F) in here,

so it's a relief when the driver finally lets out the brake and eases us onto one of Chennai's teeming streets, encouraging air to ooze through the open windows.

Public transport: you have to love it. You can't seriously say you've experienced a place until you've sampled its public transport. It's like a diorama of the city it services, a visitor's introduction to real local life. In Japan it's the bullet train. In London, a red double-decker. In New York it's the subway and in India a broken-down old bus.

And that bus right now, the one that's making achingly slow progress through Chennai, is a riot. It started the journey basically empty, but in the past half-hour has become more and more crowded, to the point where my backpack has gone from occupying its own slice of colourful velour to sitting on my lap. The seven or eight sets of staring eyes have become about 50.

Outside it's just as crazy. There's a temple in the dead centre of a busy road. You know it's a temple because there's a street sign in front of it bearing a huge exclamation mark and the word 'Temple'. Handy. The bus swerves around it, Bollywood still blasting, and almost crashes into a cow. The cow is not amused.

There's a tap on my back. I look around. 'Excuse me,' the guy sitting behind me says. 'What is your country?'

That's a standard question around here. 'Australia,' I reply.

'Oh.' He beams. 'Ricky Ponting.'

That's Australia's current cricket captain, and it's also a standard reaction. 'Yes.' I smile.

The guy looks around to his neighbour and nods, pointing at me. 'Ricky Ponting.'

It's been at least two hours and we're still making our way through the knotted streets of Chennai, seemingly no closer to Mamallapuram, the small town south of Tamil Nadu's capital. The crowd around me ebbs and flows, a parade of all walks of Indian life boarding and departing our rattling old bus.

Eventually we grind to a halt and I look at the driver: 'Mamallapuram?' He just shakes his head and jumps out onto the street.

The guy behind me taps me on the shoulder again. 'It is a breakdown. You should get off now.'

And so we all pile off the old clunker, seeking shade in a small storefront while about a million Indians crowd around the engine and speculate. Time, once again, is elastic. We could be here for hours under the corrugated iron roof waiting for our bus to fire back to life. Or it could be a few minutes.

Soon the crowd around the engine dissipates, as huge sacks of vegetables are unloaded from the roof; passengers start looking for another bus to flag down. The legendary Indian patience is waning. The Ricky Ponting fan strolls over to my perch, jabbing a finger at the busy highway. 'It's time to get another bus. Come on, I can help you.'

And he does. Pretty soon another creaky old bus has pulled up next to us, sacks of vegetables are loaded onto the roof and everyone scrambles aboard looking to claim a seat.

There's more Bollywood music blaring from the stereo, and more staring eyes. Clearly, not many Westerners get on this bus either. And again, it's probably with good reason. ●

The whole world is open to solo travellers.

The only question to consider is: how do you plan to travel around it? How will you move from city to city, from country to country? How will you traverse the place you're currently in? The options you choose will shape the sort of trip you end up having.

Maybe you'll go for a rusty old bus, like I did in southern India. Buses might not get you where you're going in a hurry, but they do give you stories; they do treat you to experiences. (And sometimes they're your only choice.) The following is a quick run-down of the major transport options available to solo travellers, with pluses and minuses for each. Weigh them up, and then make your call.

CAR

Cars are convenient, no doubt about it. They'll take you exactly where you want to go with a minimum of fuss. And there's something beautiful about the notion of a road trip. However, they're not ideal for solo travellers. To begin with, hire car rates are expensive for those going it alone. Fuel cost is also a problem when you don't have anyone to share it. Cars are not the most social forms of transport either,

given you'll be cocooned from the rest of the world, with limited opportunities to meet people.

BUS

There are buses, and there are buses. There are those that are the transport of the people, the old rattlers you'll find in developing countries around the world, colourful vehicles that are stories on four wheels. Buses like these are usually extremely cheap and extremely interesting. They're also slow, unreliable and prone to breakdowns. You'll get where you want to go – you just won't know when.

Then there are the fancy buses, the type you'll find in much of South America, and occasionally in other parts of the world. These buses look more like the business-class section of an international airline, with fully reclining seats and onboard waiter service. They're air-conditioned and comfortable. They're pricier than the old rattlers, but still affordable for those spending currency from home.

TRAIN

Trains are better than buses, generally speaking. They're faster, more reliable, more predictable and more comfortable.

Some of the world's most memorable journeys involve trains: the Trans-Siberian in Russia; any overnight train through India; the Bergen Line in Norway; the shinkansen bullet trains in Japan.

Trains are social. You're always up and about on trains, meeting people, chatting, sharing stories, sharing food. Trains can also be economical, particularly night trains, when you combine the cost of transport with the cost of accommodation, sleeping soundly to the click-clack of the wheels on the rails, before waking up in a new destination.

About the only downside I can see to trains is that sometimes they're expensive. This is especially true in Europe, where an intercity train ticket can end up costing you more than a flight. The trick is to book well in advance, and to look out for discount passes for travellers where applicable.

MOTORBIKE/SCOOTER

You want to yell with laughter. You want to scream, to cry out in fear. You want to hold your arms high in the air and shout, 'I'm king of the world!'

But that would be a bad idea because you're flying along at 80 kilometres (50 miles) per hour in what's probably a 60 (37) zone, trying not to be swamped by Sicilian traffic, trying to blend into the madness of the island, to stay afloat in a sea of commuters who seem desperate to get to wherever it is they're going as fast as possible so they can get back to doing very little.

Sicily on a scooter: is there any better way to see the place? In fact, is there any better way to see the world? It's long been a dream of mine to explore the globe astride a trusty motorised steed. Scooters are adventure, plain and simple. They force you to take things at a leisurely pace, but they're still exhilarating, still fun. You don't just see a place on a scooter, you feel it, touch it, breathe it in.

Sicily is the perfect place to begin your life of scooter adventure, enjoying the hot breeze in your face and the sun on your arms, taking in the sight of Mount Etna smoking away on one side of you, and the rich blue of the Mediterranean laid out sparkling on the other. And in front: the open road.

Is there any better way to see the world than a scooter

TUK-TUK/RICKSHAW/BAJAI/CNG

You'll find variations on the tuk-tuk – the iconic three-wheeled machines that zip through traffic at a hair-raising pace – throughout much of Asia. In Thailand and Cambodia they're called tuk-tuks, in India and Sri Lanka they're rickshaws, in Indonesia they're bajais, and in Bangladesh they're CNGs (named for the natural gas that powers them). Wherever you are, you'll find the basic experience the same. You hail one on the street, tell the driver where you're going, haggle with various levels of ferocity over the price, and then jump in and hang on for your life.

Tuk-tuks are fast, they're cheap and they're exciting. They're a genuine cultural experience, too, a window into the way locals get around town from day to day. They're also sometimes a bit of a hassle, given drivers are likely to give you the 'tourist price' and then try to persuade you to visit their cousin's jewellery store or carpet emporium, and they're also not particularly safe. But still, these are a must-try for solo travellers.

BOAT

Boats bear the distinction of being more than just transport: they're the holiday in themselves. Yes, there are plenty of boats designed purely to get you from A to B, like ferries and water taxis, and they do what they do well. For solo travellers, however, there's far more to be said for boats that are the destination. I'm talking about cruises in places like Croatia and Turkey, where backpackers and other young travellers pile on board motor yachts and then set sail for boozy good times. These are serious party boats – run by the likes of Busabout, Topdeck and G Adventures – and they're the ideal way to meet a good crew and see the sights (through the haze of a shocking hangover). There are similar cruises around the world, particularly in the Caribbean. A boat is also the only way you're going to get to Antarctica, which is one of the world's great journeys.

ELEPHANT

Don't ride elephants. It's not cool.

BICYCLE

The enjoyment derived from riding a bicycle while you're travelling will very much depend on where you are, and what sort of person you are. If you like riding bikes at home, there's a very good chance you'll enjoy doing it overseas. Bikes are cheap to run, reliable and provide a whole new way of seeing the world.

If you're in, say, Mumbai, I wouldn't recommend it. If, however, you're in a place that has a little more respect for those on two wheels – particularly in a bike-obsessed city such as Amsterdam, Copenhagen or Stockholm – then go for it. There, you're having a proper local experience, while also covering a lot of ground.

WALK

This is the simplest, easiest and cheapest way to get around a city. Walk, and you'll see everything. You'll go to places you wouldn't normally go. You'll breathe a city in. You'll taste it. You'll pick up its rhythm and get into its flow. The only time this is a bad idea for solo travellers is in certain cities at night, when safety becomes a higher priority than getting around on the cheap.

PLANE

There's a very good chance you'll fly somewhere on this solo journey of yours, and that that flight will not be one of the highlights of your holiday. Planes are fast and they're functional. They're also expensive and terrible for the environment, and you'll rarely meet anyone new. Try to keep your flights to a minimum.

Top: There's never a dull moment on North African roads

Bottom: Travel life in London, UK

CHAPTER SEVEN

TEN GREAT CITIES FOR SOLO TRAVELLERS

Opposite bottom left: Surfers hit the waves at Bondi Beach in Sydney

Opposite bottom right: The beauty of Lisbon

Top: The bright lights of big-city New York

You can go anywhere you want to.

That's one thing to bear in mind. The entire world is at your disposal as a single traveller; there's nowhere you can't survive, nowhere you won't find things to do, places to stay and people to help you along the way. There are, however, certain destinations that are more suited to the solo game than others. These are often safe destinations, and friendly destinations, but they're also places where you'll find plenty of kindred spirits, fellow travellers to bond with. You'll always have company in these cities if you decide you want it, but you'll also be safe and comfortable if you'd prefer to go it alone. In other words, the following cities are perfect for a solo adventure. •

TOKYO

Tokyo by night provides
endless avenues for
exploration

There's nowhere in the world quite like **Tokyo.**

There's nowhere of its sheer scale that has the same capacity for anonymity coupled with a friendly good nature. Nowhere seems as huge and intimidating at first glance, and yet reveals such a sense of safety once you're on the ground.

Tokyo is amazing. It has the power to constantly shock and surprise. It can cater to any whim, any desire or fetish. If you want to spend an afternoon reading a book and patting a cat, you can do it in Tokyo. If you want to hit a few baseballs and play the pinball machines, you can do it in Tokyo. If you want to go to a seedy S&M club and watch salarymen have their buttocks paddled by a leather-clad dominatrix, well, you can do it in Tokyo. This is a city of endless possibilities, allowing the full spectrum of humanity to express all its quirks and fantasies and urges.

The Japanese capital is ideal for any type of traveller, but in particular for those making their way around the world on their own. Of all Tokyo's drawcards – the history, the modern culture, the countless attractions and activities – it's the safety aspect that will perhaps most appeal to the greenest of solo travellers. Tokyo has

one of the lowest crime rates in the world, and though it may occasionally feel like a tangled web of nameless streets lined with neon and glass, there will always be someone on hand to help you find your way.

The enormity of this city is hard to overstate. Almost 14 million people live in the Tokyo prefecture, though if you take in the entire urban area, counting connected cities such as Yokohama and Kawasaki, the population shoots up to almost 38 million. That's more people than in Canada. More than in Australia. In the one metropolitan area.

If you're worried about standing out on your travels, about being noticed as the solo traveller, then fear not: Tokyo will not notice. This is a place where you can be completely anonymous. You can be as outlandish or as withdrawn as you please. You can do anything and be anyone and no one will show even the slightest concern. The city will just keep on moving, in a never-ending ebb and flow.

You will also never be short of things to do. This is a 24-hour city, where the sense of wonderment need never cease. By day, Tokyo presents a standard, if incredibly long, list of sights and attractions. You can tap into the city's history, to the Edo period when the settlement was first formed, in historic suburbs such as Asakusa, where temples tower over low-rise buildings, and shafu dress in traditional garb to pull old-style rickshaws by hand. You can sip matcha and tuck into wagashi, the often ornate Japanese sweets, at a teahouse nestled in the gardens of the Teien Art Museum; visit one of the onsen, or mineral baths, spread throughout Tokyo; and wander the grounds of the old Imperial Palace. Tokyo by day is also a great place to indulge in more modern rituals: to go clothes shopping in Shinjuku; to take in the views from Mori Art Museum, which sits 53 storeys high atop Mori Tower; to tour the vintage clothing stores and record shops in Shibuya and Shimokitazawa.

This, however, is still not Tokyo at its best. For that, you'll have to wait until the sun goes down. The Japanese novelist Haruki Murakami once wrote that 'time moves in its own special way in the middle of the night', and you'll never find this is more accurate than in Tokyo, where evenings can just disappear in a haze of beer and sake, where you might begin the night alone and end it in the company of a whole crowd of new friends and partners in crime, people who've taken you under their wings and done their utmost to show you a good time. Some evenings in Tokyo are languid and slow, spent picking over good food and enjoying time to yourself; others just vanish after taking on a life of their own, warping and bending and transporting you to the parts of the city previously unthought of and unknown.

When thinking about nightlife in the Japanese capital it's almost impossible to single out particular restaurants, or name just a few bars, or even decide on one experience. In this colossal city it's better to choose a suburb, an area that suits your evening mood, and explore it until the sun rises. Maybe it will be Roppongi, the notorious den of expat hedonism. Or Shibuya, a shopper's and gamer's paradise. Perhaps it will be the geek-friendly Akihabara, or the suit-heavy Ginza or the hipster heaven of Shimokitazawa. Each has its own special after-dark atmosphere, its own attractions and crowd.

And the best part of all: the safety net. The rate of petty theft in Tokyo is one of the lowest of any major city in the world; in fact, Tokyo topped the *Economist*'s 'Safe Cities Index' in 2017. Violent crime here is rare. There are few – if any – no-go zones. As a solo traveller in Tokyo you have the freedom to take a few more chances than you normally would, to meet new people, to try new things, to disappear down the rabbit hole that is this surprising, amazing and confounding city, comfortable in the knowledge that Tokyo is on your side. There's nowhere else in the world quite like this city. ●

WHEN TO GO

Tokyo is a year-round destination, though for the best weather, as well as annual events such as cherry blossom season (spring) and autumn foliage (which the Japanese go nuts for), aim to visit from March to May or October to December. Hanami, the annual cherry blossom festival, usually happens around April, when the magical sakura appear, and on most days you'll find the locals gathered in parks, eating and drinking and photographing the flowers. Of the other major matsuri, or festivals, the Kanda Matsuri in May is a lively, city-wide celebration, the Asakusa Sanja Matsuri, also in May, is another huge religious festival, attended by millions, and June's Sanno Matsuri is a popular parade worth timing your visit for.

Opposite: Senso-ji in Asakusa

Top left: The cherry blossoms, or "sakura", are the highlight of spring

Top right: Views from the 53rd floor of the Mori Art Museum

Bottom left: The gardens outside Teien Art Museum

Tokyo is amazing.
It has the power
to constantly shock
and surprise.

WHERE TO STAY

As you'd expect from a city this size, Tokyo has a massive range of accommodation options in various styles and pricepoints, from Western-style hostels and hotels to ryokan and minshuku – the traditional Japanese inns and guesthouses – as well as apartment rentals, capsule hotels, 'love hotels', which charge by the hour, and even comic-book stores that allow people to sleep on couches in private rooms. For solo travellers, your best bet for both socialising and keeping to a budget in this notoriously pricey city is a hostel, either in a traditional suburb such as Asakusa, or a transport hub like Shibuya.

Retrometro Backpackers, ASAKUSA

For first-timers to Tokyo, historic Asakusa makes an excellent base: from here you can walk to temples and great restaurants, wander streets filled with Edo-era buildings, and shop for everything from traditional artisanal products to plastic models of Japanese food. Retrometro is an old Japanese house and hardware shop that has been renovated into a small and friendly hostel, where the hosts – as passionate about travel as they are about providing accommodation – make an effort not just to get to know you, but to help you get to know your fellow guests.

2-19-1 Nishiasakusa, Taito-ku

www.retrometrobackpackers.com

Turn Table Hostel, SHIBUYA

This is the ideal location for those looking for a little peace and quiet, plus some sophistication in their hostel experience – but with all the craziness of Shibuya just around the corner. Turn Table feels more like a boutique hotel than a hostel, with only a few dorms alongside the ten private rooms. The owners are from the Tokushima prefecture, on the island of Shikoku, and you're likely to learn just as much about that southern outpost – all the food served for breakfast, for example, uses ingredients from Tokushima – as you are about Tokyo at this congenial little property.

10-3-3 Shinsencho, Shibuya-ku

www.turn-table-hostel-jp.book.direct

Opposite top left: Traditional Japanese sandals

Opposite top right: Mt Fuji looms on the Tokyo horizon

Opposite bottom left: The "lucky cat", one of the enduring symbols of Japan

Opposite bottom right: Lanterns advertise a shop's wares

> Tokyo has a massive range of accommodation options in various styles and pricepoints.

 ## WHERE TO EAT

There is almost literally no bad place to eat in Tokyo. From the most expensive three-Michelin-starred fine-diner to the cheapest convenience store, pretty much every dish you eat in the Japanese capital will be prepared with dedication and care. And we're not just talking sushi here. The local food runs the gamut from noodle soup (ramen) to deep-fried fish and vegetables (tempura), pancakes of cabbage, egg and noodles (okonomiyaki), and crumbed pork fillets (tonkatsu). And the pricepoints vary wildly – you could pay ¥1000 for your meal, or ¥50,000.

Solo travellers will occasionally run into problems in Tokyo, as many restaurants have very limited seating, and some high-end venues can be wary of booking a single diner, leaving a precious seat free. There is relief, though: at any ramen bar or izakaya (Japan's answer to tapas bars), or casual restaurant in train stations and shopping centres, you'll have no problem walking straight in. Plenty of other people will be doing the same.

There's never a shortage of food in this food-obsessed city

Afuri, EBISU

There are several branches of this wildly popular ramen restaurant, where the prices are low, the service is casual and the noodle soup is incredibly good. Simply order from the vending machine at the front of the store, take a ticket, grab a barstool, and hand over your order to the nearest chef. Pretty soon you'll have a steaming bowl of goodness in front of you, with plenty of pork and noodles in a hearty broth that's brightened up with yuzu, the Japanese citrus. Afuri also does an excellent vegan ramen.

1-1-7 Ebisu, Shibuya-ku

www.afuri.com

Hiroki, SHIMOKITAZAWA

The streets of trendy Shimokitazawa are lined with small bars, cafes, restaurants and izakayas, all of which get super busy at night, but are easy enough to call into for a quick bite during the day. One of the best and most affordable is Hiroki, a no-frills okonomiyaki joint that does a seriously good trade in Hiroshima-style pancakes – that is, pan-fried towers of shredded cabbage and noodles, topped with your choice of bacon, scallops, prawns or maybe oysters, plus sauce. Wash it down with a beer and you've had yourself the lunch of champions.

2-14-14 Kitazawa, Setagaya-ku

www.teppan-hiroki.com

Fuku, YOYOGI-UEHARA

You probably never dreamed that yakitori – the art of grilling chicken on small wooden skewers – could be this good. But it is. Fuku is a friendly little neighbourhood restaurant just a few stops on the train from Shibuya, and is a place where yakitori is elevated to a delicious new level. It's not only the grilled chicken that's good here, either: try the small peppers stuffed with cheese, the enoki mushrooms wrapped in bacon, or the grilled Hokkaido potatoes. All are incredibly tasty. Fuku takes bookings for its first sitting at 6.30pm, and accepts walk-ins (including solo diners) from about 8pm.

3-23-4 Nishihara, Shibuya-ku

www.sumibikushiyakifuku.com

35 Steps, SHIBUYA

Izakaya culture is every solo traveller's ticket to a good time in Tokyo. These casual, friendly bars can be found across the city, offering affordable, tasty meals, staying open late, and usually welcoming walk-ins and solo diners. You'll make friends in an izakaya, without doubt. There will always be a boozy salaryman or two keen to strike up a conversation. For a great balance of informal charm and excellent food, check out 35 Steps, an underground izakaya in bustling Shibuya where the dishes are reliably good, and the staff are reliably bonkers.

1-1 Maruyamacho, Shibuya-ku

+81 3 3770 9835

WHERE TO DRINK

Tokyo is a 24-hour city with a deep passion for nightlife. For some that means hanging out in arcade parlours or comic-book stores all night. For others it's diving into Tokyo's seedy underbelly, exploring red-light districts such as Roppongi and Kabukicho. For others still the nights are for catching live bands, or eating great food, or holing up in a tiny whisky bar and working their way through the selection. Whatever your poison, or passion, Tokyo is ideal for those going solo, a mostly safe and friendly place where every flavour of experience is ripe for the sampling.

Rather than attempt to narrow this huge city's options to just a couple of bars, I've instead detailed a few of the different styles of nightlife options available to solo travellers.

Live houses

Tokyo has a thriving live music scene, which can take time to discover given many of the venues (known as 'live houses') are tiny underground joints with bands you've probably never heard of, and unobtrusive doorways that you'd likely walk past a thousand times without noticing. However, with a little research online you'll find hundreds of gigs on any given night, everything from lounge-style jazz to hardcore punk, from cheesy J-pop to hipster-friendly alternative jams. The suburbs of Shinjuku, Shimokitazawa, Shibuya and Koenji are great places to start.

Standing bars

There's a particular style of bar in Tokyo that will always appeal to solo drinkers, as well as those on a budget: standing bars, or tachinomi, the cheapest and most casual of them all. As the name suggests, standing bars don't have seats or even barstools: patrons all stand at high tables, sipping cheap drinks and eating cheap food. These are usually rowdy, friendly joints where drinkers are in for a good time, not a long time – they'll scarf their drinks, make some friendly chatter, and be on their way. The suburb of Nakano, just west of Shinjuku, has some excellent local tachinomi on a street known as Nakano Broadway.

www.timeout.com
www.japantimes.co.jp

Whatever your
poison, or
passion, Tokyo
is ideal for those
going solo.

Whisky bars

Japan has fast become famous for
its whiskies, which have been bagging
global awards and often sell out of
stock, such is the demand. The culture
of whisky drinking is hugely popular in
Japan, particularly in Tokyo, where you'll
find many a smoky bar dedicated to its
consumption. These are often the perfect
spots for solo travellers to perch on a
barstool and watch the world go by. For a
combination of artfully curated music and
excellent whisky, check out Bar Martha in
Ebisu (www.martha-records.com), or call
into JBS in Shibuya (1-17-10 Dogenzaka)
for a dram with a side of jazz.

Top: Diners prepare to order in
an izakaya

Bottom: Convenience stores
in Japan have excellent – and
affordable – local beer selections

WHAT TO DO

Where do you start? Actually, where do you finish? There's so much to do in Tokyo, from the traditional to the modern, from the outlandish to the wholesome, that you can't possibly distil the experience into four recommendations. These tips do, however, show the range of activities on offer in this amazing city, particularly for those travelling on their own, whether they are keen to meet fellow wanderers or happy to try things by themselves.

HiSUi batto class

The term 'batto' doesn't sound very interesting, so let's run with the translation: this is essentially a sword-fighting class. Sounds better, right? HiSUi is a small studio in the business district of Ginza that offers introductory sword-wielding classes to anyone who's game. In a short session you'll learn from the masters how to draw your sword, how to ready yourself in the proper stance, and how to slice a roll of bamboo mat in half. Every movement is precise and has meaning – it's fascinating.

4-3-13 Ginza, Chuo-ku

www.en.hisui-tokyo.com

Record store crawl

Music lovers, rejoice. Tokyo is a city with a deep passion for music – and this, coupled with a love of all things old and kitsch, means record stores. Hundreds of them. Selling CDs, cassettes, vinyl records, accessories, merchandise and so much more. You could spend days trawling the record stores of Shinjuku and Shibuya and never be bored. Begin in mega-stores such as Disk Union, Tower Records or HMV, and work your way down to the tiny shops that specialise in only a few genres.

www.timeout.com

Antenna stores

It doesn't take long to realise how obsessed the Japanese are with the regional differences in their own country, especially when it comes to food: the best dairy products come from Hokkaido; the best citrus comes from Nagano; the best tofu comes from Kansai. To find out more about each prefecture, and the produce it's known for, call into an 'antenna store', a shop specialising in the food and crafts of one specific region. Ginza is ripe with these little gems, with shops representing Hiroshima, Niigata, Hokkaido, Nagano and many more. You can tour the entire country without leaving Tokyo.

www.bento.com/r-antenna.html

Shinjuku night tour

It's an intimidating beast, Shinjuku, particularly at night. This suburb is *Blade Runner* personified, a monster with neon eyes and glass and steel jaws. It's home to the bustling red-light district of Kabukicho and the ramshackle warren of tiny bars that is Golden Gai, and big-screen billboards and flashing lights line its main thoroughfares. In other words, it's huge, and you need a guide. The answer is Urban Adventures, which offers a 'Kanpai Tokyo' guided tour of Shinjuku by night: an excellent way to get to know the friendly nooks of this daunting suburb, while also getting to know fellow travellers.

www.urbanadventures.com

The streets of Shinjuku at nighttime

NEW YORK CITY

Ready to explore
in Brooklyn

Here's the annoying thing about **New York City**.

The people who live here, the ones who call this place home, seem to think the Big Apple is the centre of the universe. If it doesn't happen in NYC, then it doesn't matter. If you're not a celebrity here, you're not a celebrity anywhere. That's the attitude, and it's the sort of thing that can get on your nerves a little if you happen to reside anywhere else in the the world.

But that's not what's most annoying. What's most annoying is when you go to New York City and realise that these people are absolutely right. This really is the centre of the universe. Or, at least, it sure feels that way when you're here.

There's just so much going on in New York, so much to see, so much to do, so much that's interesting and exciting, so much that's either immediately recognisable from a million films and TV shows or hidden and waiting to be discovered. This city wears many hats – artistic centre, fine-dining capital, hipster haven, mass-tourism hotspot, fashion leader – and it balances all of them with seeming ease. You'll always find your tribe in NYC, the people or places that appeal to you. This *is* the centre of the universe.

New York is ideal for solo travellers, who will enjoy not only the safety of the city (it's seriously cleaned up its act since the bad old days of the '70s and '80s) but also the ease with which they can get around and see everything on offer. The famed subway system might not be easy to navigate at first, but most of the time it will get you to where you want to go; plus there are ferries, buses and the ubiquitous yellow cabs to take care of the rest. And, despite what you may have heard ('Hey! I'm walkin' here!'), New Yorkers are surprisingly helpful, and will likely lend a hand if you find yourself stuck. This is, after all, a city of immigrants and holiday-makers who never left, of dream-chasers and dream-livers – most residents know what it feels like to be lost and a little overwhelmed in NYC.

This is a city where you will always find company if that's what you desire. There are fellow travellers everywhere, for starters. The locals are usually happy to meet new people, and you'll find you have a foolproof ice-breaker at your disposal: your foreign accent. Speak, and people will be instantly curious. Order a drink at a bar and someone will notice you. Buy a ticket at the cinema or theatre and someone will strike up a conversation. New Yorkers are busy, sure, and they don't suffer fools gladly. But that doesn't mean they'll avoid friendly chatter when they settle in one spot.

It is also 100 per cent okay to go out and do things on your own in New York. No one will stare at you if you go out to eat at a table for one. No one gives you a second glance if you're propping up the bar with a glass of wine and a book. This is a city with a can-do mentality, where singledom, even among residents, is no barrier to getting out and enjoying everything the place has to offer. You won't stand out flying solo. If anything, it will help you blend in.

You're free to choose your poison on any given day in New York, to choose which of the city's many scenes you'd like to scout and then go deep into, get as passionate about as any New

Yorker would. Maybe it's art, in which case you can wander through gallery after gallery, from viewing the masters at MoMA to discovering new talent at 47 Canal. Maybe it's music, which can lead you from buskers in Central Park to the small venues of Brooklyn to the stadiums of Manhattan. It might be sport, in which case you would head to Yankee Stadium or Madison Square Garden. Or it could be food – and, boy, has New York got food: food from around the world, from all the cultures New York has absorbed, everything from Russian-style deli eats to Cuban sandwiches to Mexican taco stands to dirty-water hot dogs to the best pizza by the slice you've ever tasted.

New York is a kaleidoscope, a circus. It's a party and it's a playground. It's the city that never sleeps, but it's also a city that never stops moving, never stops reinventing itself, never stops innovating or taking chances or doing things no one else has thought to try. It feels like the centre of the universe. ●

New York is a kaleidoscope,
a circus. It's a party and it's
a playground.

Opposite left: Time to relax near Brooklyn Bridge

Top left: Manhattan's famous skyline

Top right: Street artists love this city

Bottom: It seems like there's pizza on every corner in New York

WHEN TO GO

You're unlikely to find a quiet time to visit New York – there's always something going on here. Christmas is an amazing time to be in the city, when you can ice-skate at the Rockefeller Center and see the lights adorning the houses. Summer, however, is when festival season really kicks off. In the warmer months (June–August) there's Shakespeare in the Park (open-air theatrical performances in Central Park), Museum Mile Festival, when the city's major museums throw a huge block party, and NYC Pride, plus a free outdoor arts festival called SummerStage, as well as film festivals, dance music festivals and plenty more.

WHERE TO STAY

New York has it all, of course. Everything from five-star luxury hotels to flea-infested boarding houses, with boutique hotels, hostels, and home and apartment rentals in between. You can stay in Manhattan – in Uptown, Midtown or Downtown, in neighbourhoods like Greenwich Village or SoHo. Or there are more adventurous places to stay and explore, such as the likes of Williamsburg in Brooklyn, the hipster enclave, and Queens, perhaps the most culturally diverse of New York's many neighbourhoods. Back in Manhattan there's the Meatpacking District, once a rough industrial area, now a nightlife hub; and Harlem, the traditional heart of NYC's African-American community. In such a huge city, it's worth identifying the area that appeals most for this particular visit and basing yourself there.

Q4 Hotel, QUEENS

Queens is a fascinating place, where walking from one city block to the next will take you from one country to another, and every culture from around the world seems to be represented in the form of a restaurant, a deli, a bar or a beer garden. Queens is also just a skip across the river from the Upper East Side of Manhattan, making it an ideal base for travellers looking to save a bit of cash. Q4 Hotel is a hostel in central Queens, with plenty of mixed and single-sex dorm rooms, as well as private rooms with ensuites. It also has plenty of communal areas, including a kitchen, a games area and a movie area.

29-09 Queens Plaza N, Long Island City

www.q4hotel.com

Jazz on the Park, UPPER WEST SIDE

Manhattan's Upper West Side is famously wealthy, and famously attractive for visitors; the neighbourhood borders Central and Riverside parks, it's home to several top-notch museums and theatres, and it's an absolute pleasure to stroll around day or night. It's also home to one of NYC's best hostels, and the ideal spot for solo travellers to stay, the Jazz on the Park. This hostel is located, as the name suggests, a stone's throw from Central Park, and has a great sociable atmosphere, particularly in summer when the staff put on barbecues and organise pub crawls. Best of all: they don't actually play that much jazz.

36 W 106th St, New York

www.jazzhostels.com

Top: Manhattan
Bridge, one of New
York's most famous
structures

Bottom: Street
art adorns the
Williamsburg walls

🌭 WHERE TO EAT

New York has always been known for its international food scene: pretty much any cuisine you could name you'll find in the Big Apple. Some of the specialties include Jewish food – bagels, pastrami, lox, blintzes, pickles – as well as great Korean barbecue in, fittingly, Koreatown, excellent Mexican and Puerto Rican food in Bushwick, Italian in Greenwich Village, African-American and West Indian in Harlem, Jamaican and Creole in Flatbush and Polish in Greenpoint. And then you have the distinctly 'New York' dishes: New York baked cheesecake, New York–style hotdogs, New York pizza and so much more. You will never go hungry in this city.

There's also, fortunately, no stigma attached to eating out alone here. Locals do it all the time, particularly in more casual restaurants and bars but even in the city's more formal eateries, some of which offer bar seating that's reserved purely for walk-ins. Solo diners will have no problem bagging a place.

Katz's Delicatessen, LOWER EAST SIDE

This place is no secret – Katz's is where Meg Ryan faked a good time in *When Harry Met Sally*, and where Johnny Depp hung out in *Donnie Brasco* – but it still bears mentioning, because the Jewish-American food here is legendary for a reason. The ordering process at Katz's is an experience in itself, involving a convoluted billing process of tickets and stamps, but it's worth it to get your hands on the famous pastrami on rye.

205 E Houston St, New York

www.katzsdelicatessen.com

Gramercy Tavern, FLATIRON DISTRICT

This is one of the truly classic New York restaurants, a Manhattan institution that's been around since the early 1990s, and these days boasts a Michelin star. The dining room is a fairly formal affair, where reservations are essential and white tablecloths are de rigueur; however, as is the trend in NYC now, there's also a far more casual bar area at the Gramercy that works on a first-in, best-dressed basis, with a pared-down and much more affordable menu.

42 E 20th St, New York

www.gramercytavern.com

Grand Central Oyster Bar, MIDTOWN

This is another NYC institution, which has been around more than a century, serving up oysters long before oysters were a thing. As the name suggests, the Grand Central Oyster Bar enjoys a prime location in Grand Central Station, which means you can combine your dining with a little sightseeing. The venue, in fact, is an attraction in itself. Don't miss the Oyster Pan Roast, which is cooked with clam juice, Worcestershire sauce and paprika. It's better than it sounds.

Grand Central Terminal, New York

www.oysterbarny.com

Gray's Papaya, UPPER WEST SIDE

This is every budget-conscious solo traveller's dream come true: for the princely sum of US$4.95, you can order Gray's famous 'Recession Special', which is two hot dogs and a soda. Goodbye hunger pangs. Gray's Papaya is an NYC favourite that has featured in plenty of films and TV shows, and holds a fond place in most New Yorkers' hearts, particularly those who've ever been students, or unemployed.

2090 Broadway, New York

www.grayspapayanyc.com

You will never go hungry in this city.

Totonno's Pizzeria, CONEY ISLAND

Ask a handful of New Yorkers where the city's best pizza is, and you'll get a handful of different answers. Everyone has their personal favourite, and the truth is that there is a lot of great pizza in NYC. Still, for one of the city's classics, head out to Coney Island and visit Totonno's, which has been serving thin-crust Napolitano pizzas for more than 90 years.

1524 Neptune Ave, Brooklyn

www.totonnosconeyisland.com

WHERE TO DRINK

Trying to boil this huge, hard-partying, 24-hour city down to a few entries, just a few bars and nightclubs, is a fool's errand. How do you choose? How do you even narrow your night down to one neighbourhood? How do you make the call between the hipster hangouts of Williamsburg, the friendly bars of the East Village, the upmarket cocktail bars of the Financial District and the dive bars of downtown Brooklyn? You can't. It's impossible.

All you can really do in New York is measure your mood and pick a neighbourhood that feels appropriate to it, decide whether you're up for cocktails or cheap beers, live music or sport on the big screen. Pretty much every bar will be suitable for solo drinkers, and you'll very likely make new friends in no time.

Attaboy,
LOWER EAST SIDE

NYC is renowned for its cocktail culture, and you can tap into that at Attaboy, a classy, cosy joint in the Lower East Side. There's a long bar here where solo patrons can pull up a stool and chat to the staff about their particular cocktail persuasions, and before long you'll have a bespoke drink in front of you, and a crowd of people to chat to.

134 Eldridge St, New York

www.attaboy.us

Union Pool,
WILLIAMSBURG

Drinking alone can be a lot of fun – the night is yours to do as you please. But sometimes it's nice to have company, to maybe meet someone you could at least spend the night with, if not the rest of your life. If that's the mood that's taking you, then head to Union Pool, a well-known pick-up joint that's filled with a friendly, though not overly seedy, crowd.

484 Union Ave, Brooklyn

www.union-pool.com

Drinking alone can be a lot of fun – the night is yours to do as you please.

Top: Cocktails are the order of the day at Attaboy

Bottom: From down-home diners to upmarket restaurants, New York is a city that loves to eat

Sweetwater Social,
GREENWICH VILLAGE

The name says it all: this is a social place to hang out, the sort of bar you might enter alone and leave at the end of the night with a whole gang of new friends. The secret is the games, from Jenga to foosball and more, which tend to bring people together, and encourage existing groups to welcome new members into their circle. Also, the drinks are cheap.

643 Broadway, New York

www.drinksweetwater.com

WHAT TO DO

Boredom is not something to fear in New York. People spend entire lifetimes here and still don't cover all the things there are to do. Once again, it will depend on your mood, on your particular goals or hankerings, as to the best way to occupy your time. There are, however, a few classic experiences that should feature on every itinerary.

Walk the High Line

Fancy a walk in a park that's almost 2.5 kilometres (1.5 miles) long but only 20 metres (65 feet) wide? Welcome to the High Line, a disused elevated railway line that runs through New York's Chelsea and Meatpacking districts. The line was abandoned back in 1980, and reopened as a park, featuring the native vegetation that had already begun to colonise the old track, in 2009. It's since become one of New York's most popular attractions.

www.thehighline.org

Check out MoMA and the Met

New York's museums and art galleries are perfect in so many ways: for the lone wanderings of solo travellers; for the budget-conscious; for escape from inclement weather; and for viewing works by the world's masters. Two of the largest and most famous are the Metropolitan Museum of Art (the Met) – featuring an entire Egyptian temple, among other things – and the Museum of Modern Art (MoMA), featuring works by Cézanne, Van Gogh, Matisse and more.

www.moma.org
www.metmuseum.org

Go cafe hopping in Williamsburg

Good news, solo travellers: New York is a city for strolling. It's the ideal place to get out there on two feet and explore neighbourhood after neighbourhood, so compact and compelling is this city. One of the best areas for strolling, particularly for those who are fans of cafe culture, is Williamsburg in Brooklyn, which has a whole host of great coffee shops nestled among the boutiques and bars and design stores.

Go to a Yankees (or Mets) game

Though the classic New York sporting experience is a baseball game at Yankee Stadium — and there's a lot to be said for going to one — there's plenty more out there for sports fans. For starters, there's a second baseball team: the Mets. They play at Citi Field in Queens. There are also two football teams (the Jets and the Giants), two basketball teams (the Knicks and the Nets), and two ice hockey teams (the Rangers and the Islanders). For tickets, go to the website below.

www.stubhub.com

Top: A busker entertains the subway crowd

Bottom: Batter up in the famed Yankee Stadium

BUENOS AIRES

Buenos Aires: one
of South America's
most beautiful
and vibrant hubs

It takes a while to get used to the rhythm of **Buenos Aires**, to figure out how this place works.

You'll call past a shop in the middle of the afternoon and it will be closed. You'll go to a popular restaurant at dinnertime and no one will be there. You'll head out to a bar at night and the place will be dead. What gives? This is supposed to be such a thriving, bustling city, a place where everyone is obsessed with fashion and good food and drink, where everyone is up for a good time, all the time. So where are they?

But that's the thing about the Argentine capital. It is all of those good things, just at different times. Many small shops and boutiques in BA won't open until late in the morning, and will then close for siesta in the mid-afternoon, and be packed with shoppers in the early evening. The only people who go out for dinner at what most of us

would consider a 'normal' time are tourists – Porteños, the citizens of Buenos Aires, eat from nine or even ten o'clock onwards. They hit the bars around midnight. They go to clubs at about two or three in the morning. They go to sleep, for a little while, and then go to work, and then go home to sleep a little longer, and then go out on the town and repeat.

For travellers, it can take a while to pick up the rhythm of this place, to begin to move in the same way the Porteños do, to embrace the soul of the city and make it their own. Once you do that, you will discover what's so great about Buenos Aires. And it is great. This is a city of passion. Just check out the dancers in the milongas, the tango clubs, and you'll see it in their faces, deep and intense. Wander the streets and enjoy the Parisian-style architecture, but watch out for the protests and strikes that regularly grind Buenos Aires to a halt – there's plenty of passion there. Listen as the hardcore fans cheer and sing and howl at a football match; it's there, too.

The passions of the Porteños are reserved solely for the good things in life. They're reserved for fashion, for looking good, for never leaving the house without a natty scarf or the perfect boots. They're reserved for food and wine, for the ubiquitous steak and Malbec, as well as influences from Italy and Spain, Peru and Japan. They're reserved for football, for a favourite team. And for family and friends, for spending time away from the office and doing what really matters: enjoying life, enjoying the city.

Solo travellers fall in love with Buenos Aires, perhaps not instantly, but certainly eternally. The Argentine capital is the best of so many worlds, a place that mixes the elegance and romanticism of Western Europe with the passion and unpredictability of South America, that is recognisable enough to be comforting, and yet foreign enough to be an adventure. It's edgy, no doubt, and sometimes gritty – pickpockets work crowded tourist zones, and the cab drivers will occasionally attempt to fleece you. But that's something to guard against, rather than let it turn you away.

The rewards in Buenos Aires are almost infinite, and the city's myriad passions are so easy to tap into, even for those visiting alone. By day you'll find yourself walking pretty, tree-lined streets, calling into sidewalk cafes for coffee and a medialuna, the Argentine croissant; you'll explore art galleries and fashion boutiques, relax over long lunches in the true Porteño style; and you'll very quickly embrace the idea of the siesta, of spending a few hours every afternoon resting and preparing for the evening ahead.

At night you'll come to love everything that Porteños love. You'll tour the shops of Palermo and San Telmo in the early evenings, grab cheap empanadas and takeaway beers on your way to the tango clubs or the friendly bars filled with locals and other travellers; you'll dance, and dance, and dance until the morning sun.

Buenos Aires has the traditional tourist attractions, if you want to find them. There are the brightly painted streets of La Boca, and there's the richly decorated cemetery in Recoleta, where the grave of Evita is a site of pilgrimage, plus plenty of museums and cultural centres. The best thing to do here, however, especially as a solo traveller, is to adopt the Porteño sensibility, to channel your energy into the good things in life, to tap into the rhythm of the city and begin to sway. ●

Opposite top left: The Casa Rosada, or 'Pink House'

Opposite top right: Empanadas: your ticket to cheap, delicious eating

Opposite bottom: Street art adorns many of the walls in Buenos Aires

Top left: The colourful streets of the Boca neighbourhood

Top right: Fashion forward in Buenos Aires

 ## WHEN TO GO

November is a great time to be in Buenos Aires. Not only is the weather good as summer approaches, but there are some excellent events to attend, including the Polo Championships, which Porteños are surprisingly passionate about, and the Festival de Tradición, a celebration of gaucho, or cowboy, culture in a rural part of the Buenos Aires province. In August, the World Tango Dance Tournament takes over the city, and it's a spectacular time to visit and soak up this authentic BA tradition. If you're a football fan, there's good news: the domestic competition only pauses during June and July. Any other time of year you'll be able to see a game.

Solo travellers fall in love with Buenos Aires, perhaps not instantly, but certainly eternally.

WHERE TO STAY

The general affordability of Buenos Aires for most travellers, even those going it alone, means a large range of accommodation options are available. While the properties listed here are hostels that are on the cheaper end of the scale, if you have a little more cash to splash there are some excellent boutique hotels in Buenos Aires, particularly in Recoleta and Palermo, that are worth it for a night or two of comfort and style.

Most of BA's budget hotels and hostels can be found in Palermo, a popular nightlife and boutique shopping district, and San Telmo, a bohemian neighbourhood that's closer to the CBD and La Boca. Both areas are safe and comfortable for solo travellers.

America del Sur, SAN TELMO

This frankly gigantic hostel has been voted the best in Argentina and the best in Latin America by Hostelworld.com users, and it really is a great venue, with the choice of small, four-bed dorms or private rooms, and plenty of social and entertainment areas. You'll find the crowd here a mixed bag, with people of all ages and nationalities, many of whom will also be travelling alone. The hostel has an excellent travel desk that can organise tours and tickets and even VIP access to certain nightclubs within the city.

Chacabuco 718, Buenos Aires

www.americahostel.com.ar

Milhouse Hostel Hipo, MICROCENTRO

Prepare yourself for Milhouse. The place bills itself as a 'party hostel', and that is exactly what you'll get. People who stay at Milhouse aren't there for a good night's sleep – they're there to make new friends, to go out on the town, and to have a good time. There are group outings to nightclubs most evenings. There are regular trips organised by the staff to tango shows, football matches and even local restaurants. It's a lot of fun – you just have to be up for it. Of the two locations in BA that Milhouse enjoys, the 'Hipo' hostel is probably the most charming, housed in a 19th-century colonial-era building.

Av. Hipolito Yrigoyen 959, Buenos Aires

www.milhousehostel.com

Top left: Hitting the streets in the Micro Centro

Top right: Buenos Aires is all about colour

Bottom: Market shopping is one of the city's great attractions

The Argentine capital is the best of so many worlds.

🥩 WHERE TO EAT

Eating in Buenos Aires is a joy, as long as you remember the correct times to do it. Have a light breakfast mid-morning, a late lunch around 2pm, then snack on alfajores – biscuits sandwiched around caramel – in the afternoon, and head out for dinner around nine or ten. The food scene in this city is very diverse, and though it focuses mainly on local cuisine, you'll find influences from France, Spain, Italy, Japan, Peru and even China.

Porteños love their meat, so prepare yourself for an onslaught of protein in BA. A typical Argentine asado, or barbecue, will include several cuts of beef – short ribs, sirloins, flanks and more – as well as sausages, and a few vegetables, if there's room. Everything is cooked over fire, on a parrilla grill, and it's cooked to perfection.

The cafés of trendy Palermo are perfect for grabbing a few medialunas and a café cortado

The Argentine Experience, PALERMO

Buenos Aires has a thriving culture of 'Puertas Cerradas', or 'closed door' restaurants, which are small, reservation-only eateries often run out of chefs' homes, or in other discreet neighbourhood buildings. The Argentine Experience is the most tourist-friendly, given it is set up purely for visitors to the city. It has a welcoming, social vibe to it, along with great food and the chance to learn a little more about Buenos Aires from the experts.

Fitz Roy 2110, Buenos Aires

www.theargentineexperience.com

Don Julio, PALERMO

No visit to Buenos Aires is complete without dining at a proper parrillada, or steakhouse. You'll find these barbecue joints across the city, some high-end, others down and dirty, but all dishing out huge chunks of fire-roasted meat to the masses. Don Julio is one of the classics, a cosy neighbourhood spot that does parrilla right, using high-quality produce and cooking it superbly. It's also not too expensive, and does tables for one.

Guatemala 4691, Buenos Aires

www.parrilladonjulio.com

La Cocina, RECOLETA

Every budget-conscious traveller's meal of choice here should be empanadas, the meat-filled pockets of pastry that are so easy to come by, and so delicious. La Cocina, in the fancy neighbourhood of Recoleta, serves up surprisingly cheap and yet high-quality empanadas from a divey little shopfront that pretty much always has a queue outside.

Av. Pueyrredon 1508, Buenos Aires

+54 11 4825 3171

Lucio, PALERMO

Breakfast in Buenos Aires is a fairly informal affair that's usually eaten on the run, or at best while sitting at a pavement cafe for a quick bite and a cortado, a strong black coffee cut with a little milk. Lucio, in Palermo, is a local favourite not just for its excellent coffee, but also for its medialunas: these small sweet croissants are devoured in their thousands daily in BA.

Av. Scalabrini Ortiz 2402, Buenos Aires

www.luciopizzaypasta.com

WHERE TO DRINK

Buenos Aires is cool, obviously. If you don't immediately get this from how everyone is dressed, you only have to check out the shops, or call into any cafe or restaurant to know this is true. And so it follows that the bars and nightclubs will be cool – and they are. It's rare you'll find a soulless pub screening football replays in this city. You're far more likely to wander into a dark hideaway where bow-tied bartenders are slinging bespoke cocktails, or a heaving nightclub that won't disgorge its sweaty crowd until the sun comes up. Buenos Aires was built for nightlife – it's affordable and enjoyable – so gather a few new friends from the hostel and get ready to lap up what this place has to offer.

878 Bar, VILLA CRESPO

This cosy little bar in the up-and-coming neighbourhood of Villa Crespo is the epitome of everything that's great about Buenos Aires nightlife. It's comfortable, it's inexpensive, it's unpretentious and yet stylish, and the drinks are excellent. Pull up a stool at the bar or relax on a couch and settle in for a long evening.

Thames 878, Buenos Aires

www.878bar.com.ar

Frank's, PALERMO

Buenos Aires has something of an obsession with the speakeasy style of bar: the more hidden and difficult to access, the better. Frank's is one of the originals, a surprisingly large bar that's only accessible via a telephone box that requires a secret password, available on the bar's Facebook page. Get the code right and a door will swing open to another world, to a warm, classy space where cocktails are the order of the night.

Arevelo 1443, Buenos Aires

+54 11 4777 6541

Buenos Aires was built for nightlife – it's affordable and enjoyable.

Top: Few cities do cosy bars better than Buenos Aires

Bottom: Cafe culture is also strong in this city

Jet Lounge, PALERMO

Once Porteños have had enough of hanging around in dark bars making small talk and sipping cocktails, they inevitably head to a nightclub (usually around 2am) to indulge their passion for dancing. Jet Lounge is one of the city's best known, an elegant place with a strict dress code that's worth adhering to for the chance to experience everything it has to offer. For a more downmarket evening with a better chance of getting in, head to Gibraltar in San Telmo (Peru 895).

Av. Costanera Rafael Obligado 4810, Buenos Aires

www.jet.com.ar

WHAT TO DO

Though there are plenty of museums and art galleries and old buildings, which you would expect in a city like Buenos Aires, this place is best enjoyed by experiencing and doing rather than by watching. And that's very easy here, with all sorts of avenues into the activities that locals hold dear, whether that's dancing, the arts or football. These experiences are fine to indulge in on your own, but you'll probably get even more out of them if you can gather a group of like-minded travellers to join you.

Learn to dance the tango

There are several ways to enjoy Porteños' obsession with the tango. One is to attend a show, which is nice, though quite expensive. Another is to go to a milonga, or tango club, which is also great, but if you don't know what you're doing you'll be a mere bystander. The last option is to learn to do this thing yourself. And you can do that at La Catedral, a milonga and tango school in Almagro, where groups of beginners are taken through their paces nightly. It's a great way to experience the passion of the dance, as well as meet people.

www.lacatedralclub.com

Visit the San Telmo antique market

If you're the type who loves picking over bric-a-brac in the hunt for treasure, then Buenos Aires is for you – and in particular, the Feria de San Telmo, a huge open-air antiques and craft market that takes over Plaza Dorrego and about 13 blocks of Defensa Street in San Telmo every Sunday. You'll find the most amazing array of bits and pieces to sift through here, with plenty of diamonds among the coal. For an even more local experience, check out La Feria de Mataderos, a folk market and fair held on Sunday afternoons in working-class Mataderos.

Opposite: No sporting experience can match seeing Boca Juniors play football at their home ground, La Bombonera

Attend a Boca Juniors game

You haven't seen anything even close to passion until you've been to a football game in Buenos Aires. The level of obsession here is almost frightening. These guys take their football seriously. There are several top-level clubs in BA; the most famous, however, and the one that provides the best spectator experience, is Boca Juniors, who play at La Bombonera in the working-class suburb of La Boca. To attend, it's best to go with a group – most hostels organise these trips, or check out the websites below.

www.bocojuniors.com.ar
www.landingpadba.com

Go on a street art tour

Thanks to a combination of Porteños' artistic flair and the city's loose laws and lax policing, there's a thriving street art scene in Buenos Aires, with works by local and well-known international artists spread across the city's walls. The easiest way to find the best of them is to join a BA Street Art tour, which leads groups through Almagro, Villa Crespo and a few other secret spots to see the good stuff.

www.buenosairesstreetart.com

QUEENSTOWN

Queenstown's Remarkables ski area provides excellent hiking terrain in the warmer months

You could go to **Queenstown** purely for the views.

You could go just to see the sparkling expanse of Lake Wakatipu laid out before you with the jagged Remarkables mountain range looming in the background, to enjoy the rolling green hills and the sharp blue skies that seem to be here in every season. Making your approach to Queenstown is worth the price of a visit alone: whether you arrive by air or by road, the mountains part to reveal at their feet a lush valley and the town perched by the lakefront.

But Queenstown has much more to offer than scenery. This little place is paradise for adventure seekers, and for backpackers. It's heaven for food lovers and wine drinkers, partygoers and fun-lovers, for those who seek to break the shackles of the everyday and try something different, something wild, something memorable. Queenstown is a fun town that attracts fun people. It's an adventure capital and a solo traveller's dream, where there is no shortage of activities that will throw you together with other adventurers from around the world.

Any activity that ends with 'ing', anything active or adventurous, you can do in Queenstown. The town first grew to prominence as a base for skiers and snowboarders, who'd travel up to nearby mountain resorts such as Coronet Peak and the Remarkables before heading back for a little après-ski in the evening. And that crowd and those activities still exist; these days, however, there are far more experiences to choose from.

This is the town that invented bungee jumping. The world's first commercial bungee, off the Kawarau Bridge, is still in operation today, and there are two other jumps nearby. Adrenalin junkies come to Queenstown for other reasons, too: for mountain-biking, which is hugely popular, jet-boating, canyoning, whitewater rafting, skydiving, quad-biking, paragliding, heli-skiing, luging, hang-gliding ... The list is almost literally endless.

More sedate activities are also on offer. You can ride the Skyline gondola to the top of a nearby peak for spectacular views, or go for a slow cycle along the lakefront paths; you can take a cruise aboard the TSS *Earnslaw*, an old steam ship that departs several times daily. You can also head out of town, by bike or bus, to wineries in the Gibbston Valley, to villages like Arrowtown or Glenorchy, or to the 'Queenstown-lite' mountain resort of Wanaka.

> Queenstown is a fun town that attracts fun people.

Queenstown itself is also a great place to just stroll around and enjoy, checking out the shops or hanging out by the lake and taking in the views. There's also lots of great food, with enough cafes, bars and pubs to keep you amused for weeks.

Several factors combine to make this small mountain town the ideal spot for solo travellers. The first is that you won't be alone. The adventure activities and the good-times vibe of Queenstown attract a large number of travellers, plenty of whom are also touring the world alone. It's a transient place – tour groups swing in and out within a few days; travellers bed down for a week and then leave; working holidaymakers do a season and move on – but it's also a very friendly place, with people from around the world up for a good time with new friends.

Most Queenstown hostels organise pub crawls and barbecues, and some have

their own bars where you can mix with fellow backpackers. Local pubs put on specials for travellers. The town's residents are laidback and sociable. Queenstown, and New Zealand on the whole, is also an extremely safe destination, where the main threat to your wellbeing is probably a whopping hangover most mornings (or, you know, a detached retina from that monster bungee jump ...). Crimes, both petty and violent, are pretty much unheard of. Solo travellers can feel safe walking the streets, going out to eat and drink, and even just stopping to take in those spectacular views that seem to assault you from every corner and every square in Queenstown.

This is a destination that looks good, feels good and is good. You'll go for a few days and stay for a few months. And there's nothing wrong with that. ●

WHEN TO GO

Traditionally, Queenstown's high season has always been winter (June–August), when the ski resorts crank into life and the ski bums descend on the town. However, that's changing, thanks in large part to the increased popularity of sports such as mountain-biking, hiking, kayaking and other warm-weather activities. Queenstown now has something to offer year-round, and you'll find it busy whenever you visit. If you're up for a celebration, the Queenstown Winter Festival, in late June, is a city-wide party to herald the beginning of the ski season, and though accommodation can be hard to come by, it's a great time to be in town.

Opposite: Queenstown is perched on the shores of Lake Wakatipu

Top left: You can't help but be swept up by the energy of this place

Top right: Paragliding is a great way to take in the scenery

Bottom: The notoriously winding road leading to the Remarkables range

Top: Snow-capped peaks of the New Zealand Alps

Bottom left: Snowboarding, one of the area's key attractions

Bottom right: Downtown Queenstown

WHERE TO STAY

Thanks to its popularity with backpackers and other younger travellers, Queenstown has a large range of budget accommodation options. There are plenty of the standard hostels, with dorms and private rooms, as well as campsites with trailers and cabins, B&Bs, self-contained hotels and motels, and apartment rentals through websites such as Airbnb. As a general rule, the further you are from the lake, and from the centre of town, the cheaper the accommodation will be, though it's probably worth spending a few extra bucks to be near the action. Skiers and snowboarders should also note there's no on-snow accommodation in the Queenstown area – everyone stays in town and commutes the half-hour or so up the mountain each day.

Adventure Q2 Hostel

This hostel is a relative newcomer, a spin-off of the ever popular Adventure Queenstown Hostel, and it's proved a massive hit, due to several factors: its location right in the centre of town, across from the Village Green (the perfect place to relax in the sun with a cold drink); its clean, comfortable rooms and lock-up storage areas; its great facilities, including kitchen, social areas and travel desk; its boutique size, with only 55 beds in the whole place; and its group activities, organised every night by the hostel team. If you're after friendly vibes and a comfortable night, this is the spot.

5 Athol St, Queenstown

www.adventureq2.co.nz

Bumbles Backpackers

If it's the views that have brought you to Queenstown, then you might as well stay somewhere that takes full advantage – and Bumbles is just such a place. The hostel enjoys a lakefront location within stumbling distance to Queenstown's bars and restaurants, and its social areas, as well as many of its dorm rooms, have incredible views of Lake Wakatipu and the snow-capped Remarkables range. This is the place to go for a quieter, more relaxed stay, but with all the action of Queenstown close by when you need it.

Cnr Lake Esplanade and Brunswick St, Queenstown

www.bumblesbackpackers.co.nz

WHERE TO EAT

Queenstown has reinvented itself in the past decade or so, moving from purely adrenalin-based attractions to something a little more refined, embracing the food obsession that has swept the Western world and using the area's excellent local produce to its advantage. There is now a lot of good food here. Some of that food is quite expensive, but plenty of the offerings will appeal to budget and solo travellers; you can get your hands on a good feed for a reasonable amount at numerous places. The Queenstown dining scene is also very receptive to single diners: there are loads of casual spots with bar seating that don't require reservations.

Fergburger

Want to find Fergburger? Don't bother looking for its sign. Just look for the queue. There's a long line of people waiting outside this famous burger joint pretty much 24 hours a day, from greasy-breakfast seekers in the early morning to midnight munchers in the eve. What draws them in are Ferg's reliably delicious burgers: everything from beef to lamb to fish to tofu to falafel, served with a stack of tasty toppings, wedged into a large bun. Grab some chips and a beer and you have yourself a meal fit for a king or queen – and one you'll probably return for several times during your stay.

42 Shotover St, Queenstown

www.fergburger.com

Botswana Butchery

Even if you're travelling on a tight budget, it's worth lashing out occasionally on a good meal, on high-quality food that's cooked to perfection. In Queenstown, Botswana Butchery should be your choice for such an outing. Shake out your cleanest clothes and head to this local institution for a meat-based feast that may include the likes of pepper-seared venison loin, slow-braised beef cheek or slow-roasted lamb shoulder for two. Pair it with a bottle of local pinot noir for the full Queenstown experience.

17 Marine Pde, Queenstown

www.botswanabutchery.co.nz

Joe's Garage

New Zealanders have a surprising obsession with coffee, particularly the espresso style pioneered in Italy and – as most locals will tell you – perfected in NZ. To get your hands on Queenstown's best cup, head to Joe's Garage, a no-frills favourite set in an old post-office sorting room. Solo travellers should pull up a stool at the bar and order a flat white (the milky coffee that both New Zealanders and Australians claim to have invented) and a bacon roll, and feel their hangovers melt away.

Searle Lane, Queenstown

www.joes.co.nz

The Cow

The Cow isn't fancy, or even especially legit. This is Italian-style food the way your totally Anglo mum used to make it (seriously – the menu here hasn't changed since 1976). Don't let that put you off, though, because when the weather is cold and your stomach is growling, there's no place in Queenstown quite like the Cow: there's always an open fire roaring, you'll find yourself stuffed onto a communal table with instant new friends, and the food is hearty and good. You can't ask for much more than that.

Cow Lane, Queenstown

+64 3 442 8588

Grab a casual seafood lunch at a Queenstown pub

WHERE TO DRINK

There's no such thing as a quiet night in Queenstown. With so many travellers constantly flowing through, as well as seasonal workers and hospitality staff hanging around town every night, there's something happening here, somewhere, Monday to Sunday. Queenstown's boozing options range from dirty backpacker bars to friendly pubs to upmarket wine bars, all of which are welcoming to solo travellers. If you feel like keeping to yourself for the night, and just enjoying a drink while jotting a few notes in the diary, it's best to head to one of the fancier cocktail bars and nurse a drink for as long as you can make it last; for raucous good times with new friends, meanwhile, simply get yourself down to any of the following establishments.

1876

This classic pub is the perfect place to kick off your evening, with plenty of budget-friendly drinks – pints of beer and glasses of wine start from NZ$5 – and moderately priced food, including specials throughout the week. It's set in Queenstown's old courthouse, and the deck out the front is pretty much the best place in town to be when the weather is warm and the sun is shining. Sociable crowd, too.

45 Ballarat St, Queenstown

www.1876.co.nz

Harry's Pool Bar

Harry's isn't famous, it isn't fancy, and it isn't even particularly nice inside. It is, however, very cheap (pints of tap beer cost NZ$6 a pop), it has a lot of pool tables and big-screen TVs playing sport, and it's a notorious hangout for both locals and travellers who are keen to meet others in a convivial environment. And, yes, that does mean making out on a couch with a stranger. The bar also does a great pizza, making it your perfect one-stop shop.

8 Brecon St, Queenstown

+64 3 441 1325

There's no such thing as a quiet night in Queenstown.

Winnie's

If sport on the big screen isn't your thing, and you'd much rather hit the dancefloor into the wee hours, then Winnie's is probably your spot. This place is an institution, and it morphs from casual diner – with the standard burgers, nachos and pizzas – to pumping nightclub, with DJs and live bands, as the evening wears on. Best of all, if it's getting a little stuffy inside, the entire roof can open up to give the dancefloor a starry ceiling.

7–9 The Mall, Queenstown

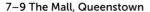
www.winnies.co.nz

Top: Lakeside in central Queenstown

Bottom: The city comes alive by night

117

▲▲ WHAT TO DO

This is Queenstown, so you're probably going to want to throw yourself off something high. Then you'll want to go down something else really fast, and then do something dangerous in some other place. That's what makes this city tick, what brings all the boys (and the girls) to the yard. Queenstown is all about adrenalin, and you'd be missing out if you didn't indulge in at least a few of its white-knuckle activities. When you've had your fill of fear, there's still plenty to keep most travellers occupied, from leisurely bike rides to gentle boat trips.

Hit the wine-tasting trail

At face value, the combination of cycling and wine-tasting may not sound like a smart one. But work with me here, because this is actually the perfect way to tour some of the Queenstown area's best wineries, while also enjoying the scenery and getting a bit of exercise. Companies such as Around the Basin, and Fork and Pedal, offer rides along gentle, custom-built bike tracks to the wineries of the Gibbston Valley area, with a van pick-up to get you back to town.

Get in the river

Several rivers snake their way through the mountainous terrain around Queenstown, and all have been put to good use in some way by various adventure companies. Around here you can go whitewater rafting, jet-boating, river-boarding or even fly fishing. Jet-boating is probably the most popular activity, and involves the least amount of work on your part: simply don a life vest and hang on tight as your pilot throws you through turns and spins in the Shotover River.

www.aroundthebasin.co.nz
www.forkandpedal.co.nz

www.shotoverjet.com

Take a hike

Though there is a gondola available to whisk people to the top of Bob's Peak, the better option for the adventurous, and the active, and the conscious-of-budget, is to hike up, which should take an hour or so, and is completely free. At the top there are options to bungee jump, to try out the luge track or to do some mountain-biking, or you can continue your walk to the top of Ben Lomond, which is a four- to six-hour round trip.

Go bungee jumping

It's a must. You can't come to the home of bungee jumping, to the adventure capital of the world, and not jump off something with a big elastic band tied to your ankles. The 43-metre (140-foot) high Kawarau Bridge is the original, and it is spectacular, but the view from The Ledge atop Bob's Peak, overlooking the lake and the mountains, is even more of a jaw-dropper, and the 47-metre (155-foot) jump here offers the extra twist of a chest harness, meaning your legs are free to take a running leap at it. For the truly brave, the Nevis bungee provides a 134-metre (440-foot) plunge into a rocky gorge.

www.bungy.co.nz

Top: The area is known for its wineries, most of which are open to visitors

Bottom: A bungee jumper is helped to safety at Kawarau Bridge

SYDNEY

The famous Sydney
Harbour Bridge

First, a confession: I don't really know what it's like to be a visitor in **Sydney**.

Not anymore. I haven't felt what newcomers to this fine city feel for at least a decade, and that's because Sydney is my home. I wake up here most mornings. I glory in the city's beaches, in its sparkling harbour and extensive green spaces, in the bars and restaurants, the pubs and clubs, in the cafes, wine bars, sporting arenas and art galleries, in everything that makes Sydney such a wonderful place to be, on the reg. I know Sydney intimately, I know what makes it tick – what it loves and hates and how to get the best out of it.

And the good news is you don't have to do much to achieve that. Sydney isn't a city like Melbourne, for example, which holds its attractions close to its chest, and requires plenty of local knowledge to discover its charms. Sydney is a little brasher and a little

bolder; everything is on display here. That harbour, those beaches, those pubs and bars and restaurants are all just there, all easy to access, all obvious and public and free to enter.

Sydney is a great city for solo travellers: I know this for sure. I know this as someone who moved here with a backpack and an air mattress 13 years ago and was forced to find his way, and as someone who has called the place home ever since. Sydney is a city that embraces newcomers, perhaps because it is made up of so many travellers and migrants from around the world, who have been drawn here to spend a few days, or weeks, or years, or even lifetimes. Sydney is multicultural and diverse, offering everything from laidback beachy good times to hipster-friendly cool, from the bleached blonde and the salty to the bearded and the tattooed. It's also a city of vast immigrant communities: Greek, Italian, Vietnamese, Thai, Portuguese, Chinese, Brazilian, and pretty much everyone in between, all of whom inhabit small pockets of the city you can explore and enjoy.

Sydney is a city where you indulge the clichés and do the obvious things because they're just so good. You would think that as a local I would have plenty of underground tips, plenty of nuggets that only Sydneysiders know, and, yes, I do. But when friends come to town I steer them – to begin with, at least – towards the popular attractions, the things that have made Sydney world-famous: Bondi Beach, the Harbour Bridge and the Opera House, the Bondi to Bronte walk, the Manly Ferry, the Northern Beaches.

These are worth seeing in their own right, but they also act as gateways to similar experiences further afield. Bondi Beach, for example, is Sydney's most famous stretch of sand, and it's a great place to hang out for a day or so, but there are more than 100 beaches in Sydney, beaches that range from surf meccas like Maroubra and Narrabeen to family-friendly stretches like Palm Beach and Bilgola and sheltered harbour beaches like Balmoral, Camp Cove and Clontarf. In the same vein, the coastal Bondi to Bronte walk is a classic, but there are so many hiking trails in Sydney. The ride on the Manly Ferry, too, could inspire you to seek

out the other ferry rides the city has to offer, from Circular Quay across to Taronga Zoo or out to Watsons Bay.

Food is a major focus in Sydney. Though there are cuisines from across the globe, perhaps every Sydneysider's favourite way to dine is going out for brunch. A meal that's supposed to be served between breakfast and lunch, this distinctly Australian obsession can be enjoyed on any given weekend until about 3pm. A Sydney brunch is a chance to sit at a cafe, drink an excellent coffee and enjoy anything from smashed avocado on toast to bacon-and-egg ramen noodles. It's also a chance to catch up with friends, soak up the sunshine and plan the night ahead.

And on that front, Sydney has much to offer. Though restrictive licensing laws have affected the city's late-night partying, there is still plenty going on in the evenings, with a burgeoning small-bar scene and a heavily entrenched pub culture. Most of the city's establishments provide a safe environment, too, with crowds that are diverse in terms of race, gender and sexual orientation.

Sydney may look a little brash at first glance, a little showy and crass. But it has a warm heart, my city, and once you discover it, you too will no longer feel like a newcomer. ●

Opposite bottom left: A surfer prepares to hit the waves

Opposite bottom right: It's always time to celebrate in Sydney

Top left: Sydney nightlife has had a resurgence

Top right: The city's numerous ocean pools are open to the public

Bottom: George Street, in Sydney's CBD

 WHEN TO GO

Being a beachy city that embraces a lust for outdoor life, Sydney is busiest in summer (December–February), when the beaches are packed during the day and the bars are crammed at night. If you're not obsessed with going for a swim, however, the city is stunning in winter (June–August), with blue skies and crisp air, and is equally lovely in the shoulder seasons. For festival-goers, there are several annual events worth building a trip around. The Sydney Festival, every January, is a three-week mix of concerts, theatrical performances and art exhibitions; March's Gay and Lesbian Mardi Gras is justifiably famous; Vivid, in May and June, is a huge festival of light that takes over the harbourfront; and Sculpture by the Sea, an open-air exhibition on the Bondi to Bronte walk every October/November, is a must for art lovers and photographers.

WHERE TO STAY

There is plenty of budget accommodation in Sydney, with backpacker hostels galore and a wealth of other cheap share options, so the main problem for most travellers will be deciding which part of the city to base themselves in. There's a glut of hostels around Central Station, which is very handy to the airport and walking distance to Chinatown, and provides easy access to Circular Quay and the Harbour. Kings Cross, meanwhile, is the former red-light district that has undergone recent gentrification, and is also easily accessible from the airport. Bondi is another popular spot, difficult to get to, and to get out of, but if you don't plan to leave – as most people in Bondi don't – then that won't be a problem. Manly is also a good alternative: a beachy, laidback suburb that's about a half-hour ferry ride from the CBD, and feels like another world.

Bounce Sydney, SURRY HILLS

Bounce is one of those hostels that just manages to get everything right: it's got the location, perched near Central Station and walking distance to bustling Crown Street in Surry Hills; it's got the facilities, with comfortable dorms and private rooms, as well as three communal lounge rooms, a TV room and a large kitchen; and it's got the vibes, with friendly, helpful staff, and organised events every night, including food and drink nights, and group outings to bars and clubs. This is your home away from home, and you'll make friends almost instantly.

28 Chalmers St, Surry Hills

www.bouncehostel.com.au

Bondi Backpackers, BONDI BEACH

Bondi is not Sydney. Or at least, it doesn't feel like the rest of Sydney. This famous suburb has a feeling all its own – everyone is tanned, toned and beautiful in Bondi. It's a hub for backpackers and travellers of all backgrounds, and a great place to base yourself if your idea of a day well spent involves sand, salt and a few beers. Bondi Backpackers does what it says on the tin, enjoying a great location right by the beach, and a large communal rooftop space to take advantage of the views (and do yoga classes). There's also free surfboard hire, and weekly social events.

110 Campbell Pde, Bondi Beach

www.bondibackpackers.com.au

... everyone is tanned, toned and beautiful in Bondi.

"

Top left: The annual *Sculptures By the Sea*, an outdoor art exhibition near Bondi Beach

Top right: Time to contemplate in Hyde Park

Bottom right: The Central Station area provides access to waterfront locales like Darling Harbour

WHERE TO EAT

Though Melbourne is Australia's culinary capital, Sydney can hold its own, particularly when it comes to affordable, delicious international cuisine. Wander a few city blocks in Sydney and you can go from Thailand to Korea, from Italy to Portugal, from Brazil to Mexico and beyond. Chinatown is the spiritual home of the affordable meal, though there are many other pockets of well-priced restaurants around Newtown, Glebe, Darlinghurst, Bondi and Coogee.

Cafe culture is huge in Sydney – on weekends, expect to find establishments across the city overflowing with patrons: groups of cyclists recharging with a quick espresso, families grabbing a bite to eat in the sun, and young people fighting off hangovers with the help of smashed avocado and a flat white. The weather in this city is usually conducive to eating and drinking outside, so expect to find plenty of people doing just that.

Top: Sydneysiders love their morning coffee

Bottom: Food, glorious food in Surry Hills

North Bondi RSL, NORTH BONDI

Bondi is filled with fashionable eateries, which benefit from million-dollar fit-outs and on-trend menus featuring chia seeds and goji berries and other things that are supposed to be good for you. North Bondi RSL has none of those things. RSL stands for 'Returned & Services League' – an organisation dedicated to Australia's defence personnel, which runs a series of clubs around the country. These are no-frills establishments with solid food and cheap booze. And at North Bondi the RSL also just happens to have one of the best views in town, overlooking the entire stretch of beach. You won't get a cheaper meal with a better outlook.

118 Ramsgate Ave, North Bondi

www.northbondirsl.com.au

Bills, VARIOUS LOCATIONS

This is one of those Sydney clichés you just have to indulge in. The city's obsession with brunch plays out as either a late breakfast or an early lunch, or even a late lunch, depending on how you spent the previous night. Probably the city's most famous brunch is served at Bills, and it's deserving of its reputation. I challenge anyone to sit down to a plate of ricotta hotcakes with banana and honeycomb butter, or Bills' creamy scrambled eggs, and disagree. There are Bills outlets in Bondi, Surry Hills and Darlinghurst.

Various locations

www.bills.com.au

Chat Thai, VARIOUS LOCATIONS

Australia has a collective fixation on Thai food that will probably come as a surprise to first-time visitors: pad thai might as well be the national dish here, it's that popular, and salt-and-pepper squid pops up on every menu from fine-diners to pubs. There are plenty of restaurants in Sydney serving excellent Thai cuisine, and one of the best is Chat Thai, which has a series of outlets throughout the city dishing up fiery, tasty, legit Thai cuisine. Pay them a visit in Circular Quay, Chinatown, Manly or the CBD – walk-ups are always welcome.

Various locations

www.chatthai.com.au

Hugos, MANLY

Like Bills, Hugos is something of a Sydney institution, and a great spot to splash out on a nice lunch if you're in Manly. Yes, there are probably better pizzas in Sydney, and definitely cheaper ones – but Hugos occupies prime position on Manly Wharf, with views of the water, and it's filled with a classic Sydney crowd (for better or worse). Grab a few drinks, share a pizza, and soak it up.

Manly Wharf, 1 E Esplanade, Manly

www.hugos.com.au

WHERE TO DRINK

Sydney has been doing it tough. The city has long struggled to take pride in a nightlife scene that has paled in comparison to Melbourne's easygoing, European-style vibe. Sydney was always more exclusive, colder, snobbier. And then along came a raft of new laws that effectively banned late-night drinking in hotspots like Kings Cross and the CBD.

However, the city is bouncing back. Cosy, independently owned small bars have begun popping up in nightlife hubs, and also in quieter, friendlier suburbs. Old music venues are closing but new ones are taking their place. Sydney is also a largely safe place to navigate on your own, the sort of city where you can prop yourself at a bar for an evening and no one will mind.

Opposite: Opera Bar, one of Sydney's best places to grab a drink

Opera Bar, CITY

Opera Bar shouldn't be this good. With a location like this, right on the lip of Circular Quay, with the famous white sails of the Opera House on one side and the coathanger Harbour Bridge on the other, it should really be a rip-off. It should be tacky and touristy. And yet the drink prices are reasonable, the crowd is friendly, and there's absolutely no better place to be at sunset. You'll find plenty of big groups here, but also lots of room for solo drinkers. Bring the camera.

Macquarie St, Sydney

www.operabar.com.au

Shady Pines Saloon, DARLINGHURST

This is the perfect example of the recent changes in Sydney's bar scene, of the slew of new small venues that ape Melbourne's classy, unpretentious drinking holes. Shady Pines has been an instant classic, an underground space with a Wild West vibe, as well as extensive beer and whisky lists. The bar is also very close to Oxford Street, which is the heart of Sydney's LGBTI scene, and a great place to hang out.

256 Crown St, Darlinghurst

www.shadypinessaloon.com

Frankie's Pizza by the Slice, CITY

This bar/music venue/pizza joint could fit into several categories here, and it has to be about the most fun place to go for a cheap eat and a tasty craft beer. Frankie's is a hard-rocking dive bar in an unlikely part of town, stuck in between the office towers and the suit-and-tie bars of the CBD; inside, however, it's all ripped jeans and Motörhead T-shirts, and the pizza is extremely good.

Icebergs, BONDI BEACH

Here's the trick to Icebergs, the restaurant and bar that occupies prime position above the ocean pool at the south end of Bondi Beach: you probably can't afford to eat here, as the prices are astronomical, but you can afford to grab a drink at the bar and nurse it for an hour or so, enjoying some of Sydney's best views. The Icebergs bar is far more casual than the restaurant, and ideal for singles.

50 Hunter St, Sydney

www.frankiespizzabytheslice.com

1 Notts Ave, Bondi Beach

www.icebergs.com.au

WHAT TO DO

Good news, solo travellers: there's plenty to do in Sydney, and many of the most famous attractions are free. Beaches are all public and free to access. National parks and gardens too. This is the sort of city where you're encouraged to walk on the grass, to sing to the birds and hug the trees. And even when the weather isn't playing the game, Sydney has enough galleries, museums and shopping arcades to keep you amused.

Head to the islands

Sydney's famous harbour is dotted with islands, many of which are accessible and safe to explore. The biggest is Cockatoo Island, previously a shipbuilding and repairs dock that has also been used as a prison and a reform school. These days it's a festival venue and accommodation site, complete with glamping tents, and it's serviced regularly by ferries. Elsewhere, there's Fort Denison, a tiny island with daily tours; Goat Island, a one-time naval base now open to the public on the first and third Sunday of each month; and Rodd Island, a small outcrop in the inner harbour accessible only by water taxi.

Take a hike

Though Sydney is famous for its beach culture, it deserves to be better known for the extensive network of national parks and nature reserves, riven with walking trails, that exist within striking distance of the city. The most famous walk is probably the coastal Bondi to Bronte track; however, it's also possible to walk all the way from Circular Quay to Manly via several national parks, or you can head north to Ku-ring-gai Chase National Park for proper bushland. All walks are perfect activities for those going it alone.

Learn to surf

With more than 100 beaches lapped by beautiful, clear water, it's no wonder surfing is so popular in Sydney – and you, too, can get involved. Learn-to-surf classes are not only ideal for meeting fellow travellers, but they're also a great way to tap into a local passion, and to pick up a skill that will stand you in good stead through the rest of Australia. There are surf schools in Bondi, Manly, Maroubra and Dee Why.

Explore the Inner West

Once you tire of the obvious attractions – the Bondi Beaches and Harbour Bridges of the world – you can move on to something different. Namely, Sydney's Inner West: edgy, interesting suburbs such as Newtown and Marrickville, Enmore and Annandale, where there's less Lycra and more lying-in, where street art adorns walls and piercings adorn faces. Go to a microbrewery: Young Henry's, or Batch, or the Grifter. Hang out at a classic pub, the likes of the Courthouse or the Vic on the Park. Go to a concert. Drink at a wine bar. This is the 'real' Sydney.

Top: Newtown, in Sydney's Inner West, provides a grittier take on city life

Bottom: Spectacular sea cliffs on the Bondi to Watsons Bay walk

HO CHI MINH CITY

The spirituality of Vietnam on display at Thien Hau Temple in Ho Chi Minh City

It's hard to know what to credit for the romance of the city once called **Saigon**.

Is it the history visible on every street, in the French-influenced architecture, the ramshackle apartment blocks, the wide, European-style boulevards and chaotic tributaries that feed them? Maybe it's the modern-day, East-meets-West buzz, the young people spilling out from bars and restaurants, the street-food stands sitting incongruously close to air-conditioned shopping malls, the cacophony of horns and shouts? Or could it just be the weather, the sultry, sweaty air that seems to hang heavy with romance?

The truth is it's impossible to say. Maybe it's all of those things. Maybe it's none. But it's hard to argue against the idea that Saigon (as the locals here still call it, despite the post-war name change) has something enticing about it, something that tempts you to visit and then pulls at you to stay. This is a city that seems custom-made for adventure travellers, for those who enjoy the rush of riding a motorbike taxi, who revel in the chance to perch on a tiny plastic stool by the side of a hectic street and slurp a $2 mystery dinner, who draw energy from chaos, and thrive on the different and sometimes bizarre.

Saigon has it all. It's big, yes, and intimidating at first. It can seem impossible to conquer, like you'll be swept up in it all, overwhelmed by its sheer force. But then you pick up the rhythm of this booming metropolis and it all starts to make sense. The people, by and large, are warm and kind. Visitors are treated well. There's true passion for good, affordable food. Even the traffic begins to make sense after a while, despite the fact it literally spills onto the pavements in some places, forcing passersby to leap away to save themselves. The city's torn history is always present, but its future looks good.

Saigon is a place you can easily enjoy by yourself; you very quickly blend into the scenery, and can go out to eat and drink and explore on your own. It's a hugely popular and affordable city for backpackers and other budget travellers, which means plenty of

> Saigon tempts you to visit and then pulls at you to stay.

chances to meet new people, too. Saigon is also largely safe, though there are the inevitable incidences of petty crime, including bag-snatchings and pickpockets, and some taxi scams. Most travellers, even those on their own, run into few problems here after taking simple safety precautions.

Once you do that, there's nothing left to do but enjoy Saigon and everything it has to offer. Some visitors will be drawn by traditional attractions such as temples and churches, which Saigon certainly has. Others will while away the days wandering through museums and galleries, which again, Saigon has in abundance. Others still will want to shop up a storm, to hit places like the sprawling, bustling Ben Thanh market to pick up a few bargains, or scour the shops in the surrounding streets for knock-off leisurewear and cheap souvenirs.

All of that is good stuff, if it's what you're into. Still, there's another, vital way in which to enjoy this city, to tap into the local psyche and enjoy the best of southern Vietnamese culture, and that is through your stomach. Saigon is obsessed with food, something you very quickly realise. There's food from all over the world, but naturally it's the local stuff that's best – some of it French-influenced, some with origins in China, but most of it purely southern Vietnamese.

It's not just the actual food that's great either, but the experience that goes along with it. To eat well in Saigon is to find yourself in some busy alleyway, sitting at a table full of strangers, slurping noodles from a bowl and trying to stay out of the way of all the scooters; to taste the cool trickle of sweetened iced coffee in the middle of a humid, busy day; to wash down good food with cold beer at a rooftop bar and enjoy this city in exactly the same way as everyone else. Before long you'll never want to leave. ●

🪷 WHEN TO GO

You can split Saigon's seasons into two neat halves: monsoon and dry.
Monsoon season lasts from May to November, and it means humid air and
some spectacular tropical downpours. From December to April, the skies
are mostly clear and the humidity is down – in other words, this is the
most comfortable time to visit. Of Saigon's holidays and festivals, Tet, the
Vietnamese New Year, usually in January or February, is the busiest, when
families across the country reunite and celebrate. In April, the King Hung
Anniversary is a nationwide celebration that involves the consumption
of a lot of rice cakes – it's an interesting time to be here, if nothing else.

Opposite: Scooters: both the scariest and best way to get around Vietnam

Top: Fresh vegetables at the market

Bottom left: Old-school apartment blocks dominate the city

Bottom right: Always a warm welcome in Ho Chi Minh City

Top left: The bustling and backpacker-friendly Pham Ngu Lao area

Top right: No-frills lakeside drinking and dining in the Mekong Delta

Bottom left: Vietnam's best street snack, the 'banh mi', or pork roll

Bottom right: Street art in Saigon

WHERE TO STAY

There's a lot to love about the budget accommodation scene in Ho Chi Minh City, where it seems like every alleyway, particularly in the backpacker-friendly Pham Ngu Lao area of District 1, offers several great options for visitors who are watching their wallets. You won't find many of the big, fancy hostel chains in Saigon — most places here are friendly, family-run establishments with only a few rooms, and perhaps not all of the modern facilities that backpackers would be used to. The idea is to lower your expectations and enjoy the ride.

In terms of areas, District 1 is the main hub of the city, where you'll find most of the tourist attractions and nightlife, and it's where most travellers end up staying, especially in Pham Ngu Lao. The southern half of District 3 is also becoming increasingly popular, and offers a slightly less touristy experience. If you're looking for a nicer hotel, the central part of District 1 is the place to go.

Vy Khanh Hostel, DISTRICT 1

This is one of the city's most popular family-run hostels, a clean, friendly place in the heart of Pham Ngu Lao that personifies everything that's good about Saigon's budget accommodation scene. The hostel has all of the mod-cons you could ask for — free wifi, air-conditioning in the dorms, laundry facilities, a TV room, travel desk and onsite cafe — as well as the sort of local knowledge and truly Vietnamese experience that you could only get from a family-run establishment.

241/11/6 Pham Ngu Lao, District 1

www.vykhanh-guesthouse.com

The Hideout, DISTRICT 1

Free beer! Really, do you need to hear any more? The price of a bed each night at the Hideout, a popular hostel in District 1, also gets you two free beers, provided you're around between 7 and 8pm to drink them. It's not a bad sweetener to what's already a great little hostel. The Hideout, once again, is in Pham Ngu Lao, walking distance to Saigon's most popular attractions, and also has a rooftop bar, a cafe, plenty of social areas, and clean dorms with lockers and power points for each bed. It's something of a party hostel, and a good place to meet fellow travellers.

275–281 Pham Ngu Lao, District 1

www.hideouthostels.asia

 ## WHERE TO EAT

The short answer is: everywhere. Pretty much every restaurant or cafe or street-food stand in this fine city offers something interesting and tasty. The people of southern Vietnam are focused on eating well – this isn't some hipster fad; it's a way of life. Food is good. You'll also find ordering a meal quite simple in most restaurants, as small establishments tend to specialise in one or two dishes, rather than attempting the full gamut. Cast your eye over what everyone else is eating, and order that.

The food in this part of the world is generally quite subtly flavoured and mildly spiced – much less of a chilli-laced punch in the face than, say, Thailand, and without a lot of the heavy oils used in Chinese cuisine. Soup is hugely popular, and you'll also find plenty of grilled meats and, unsurprisingly given Saigon's location, seafood.

Opposite: The tasty crab-based
noodle soup called bun rieu

Nguyen Canh Chan, DISTRICT 1

Tucked into a quiet corner of District 1, hidden behind packs of scooters and a big red awning, is this gem of a place that only does one dish, and does it extremely well. It's bun rieu, a rich broth of boiled, crushed freshwater crabs, mixed with noodles, roasted tomatoes, chopped banana flower, crab roe, crab meat and a hunk of congealed pig's blood. Yes, it sounds 'interesting' at best, but trust me on this: bun rieu is delicious, and this is the place to try it.

18/5 Nguyen Canh Chan, District 1

Co Lien Bo La Lot, DISTRICT 3

Up on the bustling streets of District 3, you'll spot this hole-in-the-wall joint from a mile off thanks to the smoke billowing from the charcoal grill out the front. This is where they cook the bo la lot, a finger of minced beef that's wrapped in a betel leaf, grilled and then topped with a peanut-rich sauce and wrapped again in fresh lettuce and a sheet of rice paper. It's extremely tasty, and you'd be hard-pressed to find a restaurant serving a better version than this.

321 Vo Van Tan, District 3

Oc Chi Em, DISTRICT 1

You've probably never tried oc before, and that's reasonable. It hasn't translated to the Western world. But it's a delicacy in Vietnam. 'Oc' is the local word for snails, both freshwater and saltwater varieties, and they're prepared in a range of ways at this rough-and-tumble rooftop restaurant in District 1. Again, it might sound strange, but when you're sitting down to a plate of snails fried with chilli, garlic and ginger, and sipping a cold Saigon beer, you'll understand the attraction.

3 Cong Truong Quoc Te, District 1

Banh Mi Huynh Hoa, DISTRICT 1

After pho, the ubiquitous noodle soup, Vietnam's most famous dish must surely be banh mi. This is history on a plate right here, a French-style baguette filled with pâté and pork, as well as vegetables and herbs, and topped with a tangy soy-based sauce. Saigon's best banh mi – going by the queues, anyway – is served up at Banh Mi Huynh Hoa, a no-frills joint in the northern part of District 1 that goes hard on the meat and pays scant attention to vegetables. Tasty.

26 Le Thi Rieng, District 1

WHERE TO DRINK

Ho Chi Minh City is a party town, something that might disappoint the leader who lent the city his name, but which sits pretty well with its current citizens. It's not just backpackers who go out drinking here – there's a huge expat party scene, plus a local populace that seems to enjoy a few beers and a bit of a dance or sing well beyond bedtime. As a solo traveller, you'll find Saigon a very affordable and welcoming place to go out at night, though you may benefit from getting a group together at the hostel, as safety in numbers will help you avoid any opportunistic petty crime.

Most of the places that attract a Western crowd are in District 1, where you'll find everything from pavement pubs around Bui Vien Street selling bargain-basement beers and snacks to upmarket rooftop bars peddling smart cocktails around Nguyen Hue, as well as the seedy but enjoyable nightclubs in Pham Ngu Lao.

Q Bar Saigon, DISTRICT 2

This is *the* bar in which to see and be seen, a place that is no bargain but attracts a pleasantly mixed crowd of travellers, expats and local Vietnamese. Q Bar is set in Saigon's Opera House, which was built by the French in 1898, and it retains that classic charm, albeit with a few extra neon strip lights and a better drinks selection. You wouldn't want to spend your whole night at Q Bar – it's too expensive – but this is the perfect spot to nurse a cocktail for an hour or so.

9a Ngo Quang Huy, District 2

Le Pub, DISTRICT 1

There's very little that's classy or even authentically local about Le Pub: it shamelessly courts a tourist and expat audience, though you'll still find all manner of people sprawled across the bar's three levels on any given evening. You could easily come here alone if you wanted to, but the party atmosphere does mean your chances of finding a quiet corner to read a book are slim. Better to get a crowd together from the hostel and prepare for a big one.

75 Pham Ngu Lao, District 1

Revellers enjoy
Ho Chi Minh City's
bustling nightlife

Apocalypse Now, DISTRICT 1

Yes, the name is tacky in the extreme, and the faux-military decor does nothing to raise the bar. Still, if you feel like partying in Ho Chi Minh City, if you want to dance long into the night with a mixed crowd of anyone and everyone, if you want somewhere gay-friendly and fun, if you want to wake up the next morning with a shocking headache and the feeling that you probably had a really good time last night, then Apo' is for you. Just don't say I didn't warn you.

2B Thi Sach, District 1

Trung Nguyen Café Legend, VARIOUS LOCATIONS

Granted, 'drinking' in Ho Chi Minh City usually involves alcohol. But it doesn't have to, and if you're a fan of coffee then you've come to the right place. Vietnamese coffee is some of the best in the world, and in the Trung Nguyen Café Legend chain you will find a place to relax for an hour or two, usually in air-conditioned comfort, to enjoy a caffeine hit. Make sure to order a ca phe sua da, a strong drip coffee mixed with condensed milk and poured over ice. It's good for what ails you.

Various locations around Saigon

www.trung-nguyen-online.com

WHAT TO DO

Saigon is something of a sensory overload even for experienced travellers, and often the hard part each day is choosing which of the myriad activities to go with: bargain hunting, sightseeing, eating, drinking, wandering or touring. In such a large, chaotic city it's helpful to begin your stay here with a day tour – there are plenty on offer – to get your bearings, see the places you'd like to come back to, plus chat with someone experienced about the way the city works. Talk to the travel desk at your hostel and they'll be able to suggest a few options. After that, the city is all yours.

Take a Saigon Buddy Tour

There are a tonne of companies offering motorbike tours of Saigon – it's one of the most thrilling ways to see the city, and certainly the option preferred by the locals – and Saigon Buddy Tours is one of the most highly rated. Jump on the back of a scooter and cruise through the city's highlights, or concentrate on sampling street food, or even check out some of Saigon's best microbreweries. The 'buddies' – local Vietnamese tour guides – are all very friendly and knowledgeable, and speak excellent English.

www.saigonbuddytours.com

Check out the War Remnants Museum

Though museum visits don't always offer the best window to local culture, Ho Chi Minh City's War Remnants Museum is a different beast. Take everything you thought you knew about the 'Vietnam War' and flip it on its head: this is a propaganda-soaked paean to the heroes and villains of the American War, and the Allies don't come out looking too angelic (this used to be called the Museum of Chinese and American War Crimes). Good to see the other side of the story.

www.warremnantsmuseum.com

Get out of District 1

This is your challenge for Saigon. Though it's very easy to confine your stay in the city to District 1, where you'll find the bulk of the sights, accommodation and tourist-friendly bars and restaurants, for a hit of the 'real' Saigon you need to get yourself further afield. There's plenty of laidback charm, and expat bars, in District 2, great restaurants in District 3, local nightlife in District 4 and the huge Binh Tay market in District 5. All are worth exploring.

Head to the Delta

You'll find plenty to do in Saigon itself, but it's also worth putting aside a day to get down to the Mekong Delta to see a completely different side to Vietnam. Urban Adventures runs a day tour from Saigon to the bustling delta port city of My Tho, where you can take a short cruise on the Mekong River, feast on traditional cuisine at a local restaurant, visit a few markets and experience the more relaxed pace in this part of the world.

www.urbanadventures.com

Top: Tour company Easy Riders provides a great way to get around southern Vietnam on two wheels

Bottom: Life lived on the water in the Mekong Delta

ESFAHAN

Esfahan's 17th-century
Si-o-Seh Bridge is a popular
spot for an evening stroll

I'm not the first person to fall hard for **Esfahan**.

There's a long line of poets and writers, explorers and adventurers who have already proclaimed their love for this Iranian beauty. In the 16th century one of those admirers coined the famous rhyme: 'Esfahan nesf-e jahan', meaning 'Esfahan is half the world'. But that's almost doing the place a disservice. Because if you spend just one evening in Esfahan, perched on a bench in Naqsh-e Jahan, the city's archway-lined main square, you discover that the former Persian capital doesn't seem merely half the world, but a world all of its own.

You can see so much in this square in a single evening, as the sun goes down and the world goes by. Merchants hurry through the arched stone promenades that hug the sides of the square. Schoolkids pose for photos in front of the fountains. Muezzins make their way to the mosques, to call people to prayer. Women huddle side by side on benches, chatting in the slowly fading light.

And you can meet people. You can meet so many people: groups of students who might offer to take you on a tour of a local mosque; salesmen from the nearby shops who walk over not for business but to say 'Welcome to Iran'; young people who just want to chat, to find out who you are, where you come from, what you think of their country, what you think of the world.

And the greatest thing about Esfahan? Its people are genuine. They really will want to welcome you to their country. They will want to show off their mosque, get to know you, and maybe take you to drink tea, or even invite you to their house for dinner. There are rarely any tricks or scams. Just warmth and hospitality.

I have done and seen all of these things in Esfahan. I've seen the intricate tile work in Masjed-e Imam mosque, whose blue dome towers over the square, led by a group of schoolchildren, jostling to show off their English. I've joined a local guy called Hamid for dinner in the Armenian Quarter, one of the more liberal sections of the city, before sipping tea in the palatial grounds of an old hotel. I've finished an evening down by Si-o-Seh, a huge old bridge, staring at its orange-lit arches twinkling far into the distance, watching as people came and went, played and yelled.

Esfahan is beautiful, truly beautiful, from its palaces and gardens to its mosques and bridges and squares. But, as with any love affair, it's not looks that are most important in Esfahan. It's the city's personality that made me fall for it, and makes me long to return.

You may have thought, at the start of this chapter, that Esfahan was a strange choice, that Iran in general was a strange inclusion in a solo travellers' handbook. And I understand that. Iran is supposed to be the enemy of the West, part of the Axis of Evil, the supporter of terror and developer of nuclear weapons. And who knows, maybe it really is all of those things – or its government, at least.

But that's not something that you as a traveller will ever have to worry about, or will likely believe. In reality, there can't be a friendlier place on earth than Iran, no other country where you are more likely to meet local people and make local friends as a solo traveller. Iran is safe, and welcoming, and enjoyable. And Esfahan is the best of it.

Just visit Naqsh-e Jahan and you will know this is true. Wander past an ancient mosque or madrasah, the religious monuments clad spectacularly in hand-painted tiles, and you will know it's true. Spend a night at a restaurant in the Armenian Quarter or walk across one of the city's eleven bridges, or shop in the old covered bazaar, or relax in the gardens of an old palace, and you will know, without doubt, that this is true.

Esfahan is eminently affordable for solo travellers, as is the rest of Iran. It's a place where you can stay anywhere from a small guesthouse to a large mansion and not break the bank. You can eat at restaurants, shop for high-quality souvenirs and take taxis between sites and still keep to a strict budget. The people of Esfahan are keen to show off the beauty of their ancient city, but also desperate to show the world the other side of Iran, the side that never gets covered in the news: the hospitable, warm side that will surprise and move you again, and again, and again.

If it's adventure you seek, and history, and tradition, and the feeling of exoticism that can only come from taking a step off the beaten track, from taking a chance on somewhere different, then Esfahan is for you. It won't be long before you fall in love. ●

WHEN TO GO

It doesn't often rain in Esfahan – we're talking an average of only 13 inclement days a year – which is good news for travellers. It does, however, get uncomfortably hot from June to August, and quite cold in December and January. The optimum time to visit is March, when the weather is cool and dry, and the locals are celebrating Nowruz, the Persian New Year. This festival runs for a fortnight, and includes the Zoroastrian-rooted Chaharshanbe Suri, or Red Wednesday celebration, New Year's Day itself and Sizdeh Bedar, when families take to Esfahan's parks and squares to have picnics and celebrate Nowruz's final day.

Bottom left: The tiled interior of the Abbasi Great Mosque

Bottom right: Traditional Persian tiling adorns the walls of a mosque

Can women travel solo in Iran?

The short answer to this question is yes: if you're a woman planning to travel the world on your own, you can visit Iran. You will have to dress in a way that locals consider appropriate, which means having your hair and your arms and legs covered at all times in public, but aside from that you're able to move through the country – staying in hotels, eating out, using public transport – as you would anywhere else. In fact, some aspects of life might even be easier. There are taxi services reserved solely for women in Iran's larger cities, and women-only carriages on the subway in Tehran, and bus drivers will ensure you're not seated next to men you don't know on long-distance journeys.

As a solo female traveller in Iran, however, you will attract attention. There might be other foreign women travelling on their own, but not many. You will be an oddity, which tends to attract attention anywhere, some of it unwanted. There may be the odd interaction with local men that makes you uncomfortable, including verbal harassment, but most women who've tackled the country alone report a positive experience. Women are very much a part of public life in Iran, and if you dress to local standards and act respectfully, you're likely to receive a warm welcome, particularly from local women and girls who will be very interested to hear your story and share their culture.

Top: The Abbasi Great Mosque visible across Naqsh e Jahan Square

Bottom: Men gather to socialise under the city's ancient bridges

WHERE TO STAY

Esfahan has a great range of accommodation for travellers of all budgets, and plenty that will appeal to solo travellers. Though the city does have its share of fairly bland, cookie-cutter hotels, there's also an extensive network of homestay and B&B options (at time of writing these weren't available to holders of British, US or Canadian passports, however), as well as some higher-priced hotels set in beautifully restored old mansions and even palaces. In general, you'll want to stay as close to Naqsh-e Jahan as possible, as that's really the epicentre of the city. As an alternative, Jolfa – otherwise known as the Armenian Quarter – is a buzzy spot that's filled with restaurants and cafes, and is close to the river.

Anar Guesthouse, JOLFA

Anar is the perfect archetype of the Esfahan guesthouse, a cosy, friendly space that works as a base for travellers who want to experience Iranian life and hospitality while also being close to the action. The facilities are fairly basic, with a four-bed dorm and a few private rooms with shared bathrooms, but the price is very reasonable and, really, a stay here is more of a cultural experience, as you'll be spending time with the owner, Mashad, and her family – who promise to take their guests along to any local weddings or events they're invited to.

492, 29th Alley, N Sheikh Sadoogh St, Esfahan

www.hostelworld.com

Dibai House, OLD QUARTER

For a step up in style – and price – check out Dibai House, a friendly hotel and guesthouse set in a restored 17th-century Persian mansion in Esfahan's Old Quarter. Again, this is a family-run establishment, but everything is a little fancier here than at Anar, from the cool and brightly painted social areas to rooms with mod cons. Dibai is still a social spot, though, where you can make use of a shared kitchen and living room, hang out in one of the two outdoor courtyards or attend one of the hotel's cooking classes.

1 Masjed Ali Alley, Harunie, Esfahan

www.dibaihouse.com

Top left: The old bridges
provide plenty of nooks for
quiet contemplation

Top right: Allahverdi Khan,
one of Esfahan's many bridges

Bottom left: The 1000-year-old
Bazar-e Bozorg

Bottom right: Scarves for sale
in Bazar-e Bozorg

 # WHERE TO EAT

There's something strange about Iran: this country has a strong and sophisticated food culture, with a huge range of dishes that have been perfected over hundreds, if not thousands, of years; what it doesn't appear to have, however, is a whole lot of restaurants. There are a few reasons for this. One is that there isn't an ingrained eating-out culture in Iran. Most of the country's best food is served in people's homes, so why go out to eat? Another reason is that many of the smaller, family-run eateries in Esfahan have little to no signage, and are tucked away down alleys, or in basement rooms, so in fact there are actually far more restaurants than many visitors realise. The trick is to follow your nose (and everyone else) around meal times.

The good news is that food in Esfahan is generally fairly cheap, and restaurants are welcoming to solo diners. Kebabs and other meat dishes are eternally popular in Iran, so if you're vegetarian or vegan, you'd better get used to eating a lot of aubergine.

Top: Street vendors dish up affordable snacks

Bottom: It's a world of colour and spice in Esfahan's bazaar

Abbasi Teahouse & Restaurant, OLD QUARTER

You might not be able to afford to stay at Abbasi – a luxurious hotel set in a 300-year-old caravanserai – but you can probably afford a bite to eat at its teahouse, which enjoys a lovely location in the hotel's main courtyard and garden (don't go to the main restaurant, though, it's far too expensive). The specialty at the teahouse is ash reshte, which is a hearty noodle soup with beans and vegetables. Order a steaming bowl, finish your meal off with a cup of sweet Persian tea, and soak up the surroundings without breaking the bank.

Amadegah St, Charharbagh-e-Abbasi Ave, Esfahan

www.abbasihotel.ir

Khan Gostar, JOLFA

Spend any decent length of time in Iran and you'll inevitably get sick of the standard kebabs and rice, which are served pretty much everywhere. For relief in Esfahan, check out Khan Gostar, a restaurant housed in the Jolfa Hotel that specialises in a dish called koresht mast. This tasty treat is a thick, rich stew made with saffron, yoghurt, beef or mutton, eggs and sugar. Sounds weird and looks even weirder – it's basically a bowl of bright yellow goo – but certainly worth a try.

Hakim Nezami St, Jolfa

031-1627-8989

Restaurant Shahrzad, OLD QUARTER

Plenty of restaurants in Iran serve their food buffet style, which may seem a little disappointing at first but is actually a great way to sample as many dishes as possible (and, if you're on a tight budget, fill yourself to bursting). Restaurant Shahrzad does one of the best buffets in Esfahan, as well as offering an à la carte selection if you're not feeling all that ravenous. This is a friendly, bustling place pretty close to Naqsh-e Jahan, and though it's not about to win any Michelin stars, it does provide a nice intro to Persian cuisine.

Abbas Abad St, Esfahan

031-3220-4490

Azam Beryani, OLD QUARTER

If you're looking for a proper local Esfahan experience, with good, authentic food and a friendly crowd, Azam Beryani is your spot. The specialty here is beryani, a typical local dish of grilled minced lamb that's served with fresh flatbread and a herby side salad. It's cheap, no-fuss cuisine at its finest. Don't worry too much about whether they'll get your order right, either – they only do one thing.

Masjed Seyyed St, Esfahan

031-1212-5730

🫖 WHERE TO DRINK

This might come as something of a disappointment, but drinking isn't on the cards in Esfahan. Iran has a countrywide ban on alcohol, which means the hardest thing you're likely to consume is caffeine. That doesn't mean Iranians don't socialise over a drink. Tea is a cherished staple here – hot, sweet tea served in tulip-shaped glasses – as popular in people's homes as a form of welcome as it is in the teahouses that dot Esfahan, gathering places as old as the city itself. Esfahan also has a growing number of Western-style coffee shops, particularly in Jolfa, where young people hang out and chat. And the best thing about a night out in Esfahan? No hangover.

Azadegan Teahouse, OLD QUARTER

This is a classic Esfahan teahouse, hidden down the end of a passageway lined with antique shops, its tables packed with locals drinking tea and gesticulating, its walls and ceiling lined with old teapots and other bric-a-brac. The menu at Azadegan, near Naqsh-e Jahan, is pretty limited: we're talking tea and dizi, a hearty Persian soup. You don't come here for the food, though; you come here for the social occasion, and as a solo traveller you're bound to be welcomed into a group.

Chah Haj Mirza Alley, Emam Square, Esfahan

031-3221-1225

Firouz Sherbat, JOLFA

This family-owned Armenian restaurant is set, unsurprisingly, in the Armenian Quarter, and serves up excellent coffee, ice-cream and snacks in a beautiful old building. Though Firouz Sherbat is ostensibly all about the coffee, they also do a lemon sherbet drink to cool you down on a typically hot day, and the saffron-honey ice-cream is a must. This is a homey, comfortable spot you'll definitely return to.

Jolfa St, Esfahan

031-3626-8009

> Tea is a cherished staple here – hot, sweet tea served in tulip-shaped glasses.

Top: Bargain hunting in Bazar-e Bozorg

Bottom: Always time for a tea or coffee break

Sibil Coffee, OLD QUARTER

Those missing good, European-style espresso should head straight to Sibil for their daily hit. The cafe is just near Naqsh-e Jahan, making it a handy stop-off point on your way out for the day (most hotel coffee in Iran is fairly average). There are cold drinks available here, and snacks as well, but really this place is all about getting your espresso or cappuccino fix.

Ostandari St, near Posht Matbakh Alley, Esfahan

031-3222-7855

WHAT TO DO

There's beauty in Esfahan, undoubtedly, and the bulk of your time in this city will be spent appreciating it. By all means, set aside time to see mosques and churches, to wander bazaars and spend time in the squares. But leave time to explore Esfahan's humanity: take the chance to share tea with a stranger, or have dinner with new friends, or just stop to talk to all the people who will want to get to know you.

Go mosque-hopping

The saying 'Esfahan is half the world' was never about the city's population, or even its global importance; it was about its beauty. Half of the world's most beautiful buildings exist in Esfahan, or so the locals would have you think. It's hard to argue, too, once you begin walking this magnificent city, and take in the spectacular mosques that surround Naqsh-e Jahan, and the intricate beauty of the hand-painted tiles that seem to drip from bold, brilliant archways. Most of Esfahan's 17th-century mosques – including the heritage-listed Imam Mosque – are open to the public and free to enter. Take a camera.

Walk the Zayanderud riverbank

There are few better ways to spend an afternoon and evening than wandering the banks of Esfahan's Zayanderud River. This is where the city's residents come to play, to relax with picnics, and spend time with family and friends. It's also where you'll find Esfahan's spectacular bridges, ancient pedestrian walkways that date as far back as the 7th century. On any given evening the likes of Shahrestan, Khaju and Si-o-Seh bridges are packed with locals strolling, chatting, drinking tea or just hanging out in each bridge's dimly lit interior.

Discover new religions

Though Iran these days is an Islamic republic, there are still minority religions that exist, and they can be explored in Esfahan. Jolfa, the Armenian Quarter, is home to the bulk of the city's Christian population, and the 17th-century Vank Cathedral is a popular tourist sight. More interestingly, Esfahan is still one of the major seats of the Zoroastrian religion, and Atashgar, a reconstructed fire temple, is open to visitors.

Wander Bazar-e Bozorg

Maybe you don't want to buy a carpet – if you do, though, you're in the right place. Regardless, you should visit Bazar-e Bozorg, Esfahan's oldest shopping district, a maze-like series of covered walkways beginning at the northern end of Naqsh-e Jahan. In this old market, parts of which are more than a thousand years old, you'll find everything from tea and spices to traditional lanterns and Persian carpets. You'll have to haggle over prices, but this is a welcoming space, and the perfect way to observe Esfahan life as it's been lived for centuries.

Top: The spectacular entrance to the Imam Mosque

Bottom: Traditional Persian carpets for sale in Bazar-e Bozorg

BERLIN

The Berlin Wall continues to define this city, many years after its fall

Something amazing has taken place in **Berlin**, and you can trace it all the way back to the bad old days of a divided land.

Berlin was once famously cleaved in two by a wall, a barrier that separated West from East, democracy from communism, prosperity from survival. The city in those days was filled with spies and informants, heroes and traitors. It was the site of so much struggle and pain.

And then the Berlin Wall came down, and everything changed. The Berlin of today is unrecognisable from the city it once was – it's united and peaceful, modern and safe – and yet everything that makes it so good and so exciting is linked to those divided days. The Berlin that fills you with hope and joy is a direct result of that struggle and pain.

Modern-day Berlin is an artistic hub. It's creative and free, a welcoming space for visual artists and musicians, writers and performers. And this isn't in spite of the wall, and those days of repression, but because of it, and because of its downfall.

When the old East collapsed back in 1989, the residents of suburbs like Friedrichshain and Prenzlauer Berg

fled to the west of Berlin, scared their freedom wouldn't last, abandoning their homes. Apartment blocks stood empty. Warehouses were disused. Soon, however, those empty spaces began to fill with artists and other creatives, who set up squats and sought to harness the spirit of hope running through the city, to turn it into something beautiful.

They did, and their efforts continue today. Though Berlin is changing and the creep of gentrification is claiming some of those dishevelled old areas, there are still artistic hubs in Friedrichshain and Prenzlauer Berg, as well as in Kreuzberg and Mitte, areas where you'll find counter-culture clubs and community-based movements, and small art galleries lining the streets.

Berlin's past struggles continue to shape its current mindset. Perhaps it's a reaction to the tyranny, to the former culture of suspicion and fear, but Berlin these days is incredibly tolerant and open-minded, the sort of city where anything goes – where anything, in fact, is encouraged. Whatever your kink or fetish or desire, you'll find somewhere in Berlin that caters to it. You're free to be as weird and experimental as you like in this city.

Berlin isn't Germany. Ask anyone inside or out of the city and they'll tell you that. Though Germany on the whole has a reputation for being slightly stiff and stand-offish, conservative and proper, Berlin is none of those things. It's artistic, offbeat and fun.

It feels as if every part of Berlin's modern culture and identity is intrinsically linked to its recent past. You can spot it on the walls of Berlin's buildings, in the street art and graffiti that adorns most spaces. Berliners always used to scrawl on that most hated of walls, to draw and spray pictures and messages on the structure that divided them. And that habit survived the wall: you can now see works by some of the world's most famous artists on many walls as you stroll through the city.

Berlin's history, too, appears on its menus. There's some amazingly good Turkish food in this city, with doner kebabs on almost every corner. There's also excellent Russian cuisine, as well as cross-cultural hybrids like currywurst, German sausages doused in curry sauce and paprika, which are devoured by post-party revellers across the city. Good news, too, if you're a vegetarian or vegan, as the German capital has one of the best plant-based dining scenes in the world.

Berlin is gritty, but it can also be beautiful. There's history in the Brandenburg Gate and the Reichstag, Renaissance architecture on Museum Island, and picture-perfect, boutique-lined streets in Schöneberg, Spandau and Wilmersdorf. There are plenty of historical monuments and world-class museums here too: sites that acknowledge the horror of the Nazi era, to display Germany's dark past in a bid to ensure it is never repeated.

But that, to me, is not the Berlin that's unique, nor the Berlin to fall in love with. The exciting Berlin, the 'real' Berlin, is in the streets of the old East, where nightclubs still heat up abandoned warehouses, and cheap, friendly cafes and restaurants abound, where community is valued over financial prosperity, and everyone is accepted and anything goes. This is the Berlin to dive into and explore, to soak up and enjoy.

Solo travellers will feel welcome in these places, in the same way everyone does. You'll find many locals drinking coffee alone, eating meals alone, even going drinking alone. And there are always fellow travellers around to explore this ever-popular destination with. Berlin is generally safe and simple to navigate, a pleasure to stroll and discover. The main danger, in fact, is being so taken with the joy of it, with its hope and acceptance, that you'll never want to leave. ●

Opposite top left: It's always beer o'clock

Opposite top right: The sky's the limit in this open-minded city

Opposite bottom left: Teufelsberg, the former US listening station

Top: Alexanderplatz, one of the hearts of modern Berlin

Bottom: Graffiti adorns a section of the Berlin Wall at Mauerpark

 ## WHEN TO GO

Berlin is a city that loves a celebration, so you can expect to find some sort of event on here at pretty much any time of year. Some of the bigger and more enjoyable festivals include the Eat! Berlin food festival in February, the Karneval der Kulturen in May, the International Berlin Beer Festival in August, Lollapalooza in September and the Festival of Lights in October. As with many European cities, Berlin is generally best in the warmer months (May–September), when the days are long and locals are always up for a celebration. The big exception, however, is New Year's Eve, which is mental (in a good way).

WHERE TO STAY

Thanks to Berlin's arty nature, as well as its affordability, there's no shortage of high-quality backpacker accommodation spread across the city. These hostels and guesthouses are usually modern and clean, with great facilities, interesting decor and a good crowd of fellow travellers. Berlin also has a huge range of other options for solo travellers, including a large Couchsurfing community and the chance to rent rooms with locals via Airbnb and similar websites.

Though the wall came down some 30 years ago, the city is still split into east and west, with most of the backpacker-friendly accommodation in the former East. That means neighbourhoods such as Mitte and Prenzlauer Berg, which are close to all the action – the major historical sites, as well as more modern attractions – and are filled with affordable restaurants and bars.

EastSeven Berlin Hostel, PRENZLAUER BERG

EastSeven has been voted Germany's best hostel three times by users of the Hostelworld website, and it's pretty easy to see why: this is a clean, modern space with great facilities, including beds with reading lights, power points and lockers, shared social spaces such as a kitchen, a lounge and a garden, bike rental and laundry service. This is not, however, a party hostel – it's more a home away from home, in trendy Prenzlauer Berg, and it's the perfect base from which to explore the city.

Schwedter Strasse 7, Berlin

www.eastseven.de

Lekkerurlaub, KREUZBERG

If you're after homey vibes in one of Berlin's best locations, Lekkerurlaub is for you. This friendly guesthouse is nestled between Kreuzberg and Neukölln, the twin hearts of the city's counterculture, and the kind of area you are most definitely going to want to spend some time in. Lekkerurlaub itself feels more like a house than a hostel, with just a few modest but comfortable rooms, a lounge and dining area, and a small terrace. The real attraction, however, is the arty and fascinating area it resides in.

Graefestrasse 89, Berlin

www.hostel-lekkerurlaub.de

> Berlin is a city that loves a celebration.

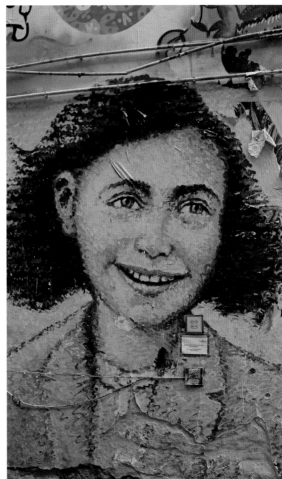

Top left: Gritty streets of the German capital

Top right: Berlin is covered in street art, including this mural of Anne Frank in Mitte

Bottom right: Berlin's U-Bahn system is ideal for getting around on the cheap

WHERE TO EAT

For a European capital, Berlin has a pleasingly multicultural dining scene, thanks in large part to various immigrant communities, as well as a dynamic modern scene. You'll find all of the German classics here – bratwurst, schnitzel and pretzels – being dished out in pubs and beer gardens, but you'll also find excellent Turkish cuisine, great South and Central American food, plenty of good American-style burgers and even Australian-style brunch. Most food in Berlin is cheap and approachable, making it ideal for solo travellers to get out and get tasting.

Pretzels and sausages:
you can't go wrong

Rogacki, CHARLOTTENBURG

Berlin doesn't have a lot of classic, traditional eateries, but Rogacki is one of them, and it's a must-visit. This smokehouse and delicatessen has been operating for almost 100 years, and it's still busy day in, day out. We're talking smoked fish, cured meats, sausages, pickles, salads and more. All of it is available to take away, but it's much better to grab a seat, take your time and soak up the old-world atmosphere.

Wilmersdorfer Strasse 145, Berlin

www.rogacki.de

Konnopke's Imbiss, PRENZLAUER BERG

Back in 1930, Max Konnopke opened a snack stand underneath the railway tracks by the Eberswalder Strasse U-Bahn station, and it's still going strong. This is one of the best places in Berlin to try a currywurst, that odd combination of German pork sausage and mystery curry sauce, paired with fries and a cheap beer. You'll eat these delicacies standing outside on the street, probably at a high table, and probably surrounded by a lot of other people doing the same.

Schönhauser Allee 44, Berlin

www.konnopke-imbiss.de

Rüyam Gemüse Kebab, SCHÖNEBURG

In post–World War II Berlin, the wall had gone up, and the West Germans needed labour to help rebuild their half of the city. Enter the Turks, who were invited in on short-term 'guest worker' visas, but ended up staying much longer. The most obvious sign of that migration is in the proliferation of good, cheap Turkish restaurants in Berlin, and there's perhaps none as good or as cheap as Rüyam Gemüse in Schöneburg. Grab a chicken doner – you won't regret it.

Hauptstrasse 133, Berlin

Pasternak, PRENZLAUER BERG

For four decades, East Germany was part of the Soviet Occupation Zone, and even now there are small remnants of Russian culture if you look hard enough. One of the easiest to access is Pasternak, a Russian-Jewish restaurant in Prenzlauer Berg that does a mean Sunday brunch buffet – perfect for the hungry solo traveller. Enjoy borsch, pickled herring, sweets, cakes and more, surrounded by a large crowd of your new best friends.

Knaackstrasse 22, Berlin

www.restaurant-pasternak.de

WHERE TO DRINK

This section could be so much longer. You could fill this entire book with reviews of great places to go drinking in Berlin, so wide and diverse is the nightlife scene. And it's all so friendly and approachable too, so lacking in pretension and aggression. Most of the places I've chosen are the more relaxed, social venues, perfect for meeting people or heading out with new friends. I haven't even touched on the hard-partying scene, which takes in legendary super-clubs such as Berghain and Sisyphos, or the live music scene, at venues like SO36 and Junction Bar, or the gay scene, or the punk scene, or the kink scene, or just about anything else you could imagine. You'll just have to get out and explore – and fear not, singles are always welcome.

Klunkerkranich, NEUKÖLLN

In a city that's essentially flat, with few tall buildings and even fewer hilltops or natural rises, it's rare to find a bar with a view – but Klunkerkranich has one. This open-air bar is difficult to find, given it's perched on the top of a parking garage in central Neukölln, with no signage. Find your way up, however, and you'll be treated to Berlin's best sunset viewing point, as well as a relaxed, sociable crowd who are usually up for drinking into the early hours.

Karl-Marx-Strasse 66, Berlin

www.klunkerkranich.de

Café am Neuen See, TIERGARTEN

No one does a beer garden like the Germans, and even in an industrial city such as Berlin you'll still find pleasant spots to sit out in the sun and work your way through a few enormous local brews. Café am Neuen See is the ideal place to while away a long summer's evening, perched as it is in the heart of the Tiergarten park, under tall trees, on the banks of a lake. The beer is cold and the crowd is friendly. Enjoy.

Lichtensteinallee 2, Berlin

www.cafeamneuensee.de

A mural at the East Side Gallery, part of the Berlin Wall that has been converted into an open-air exhibition

Prater Garten, PRENZLAUER BERG

Speaking of beer gardens, this is Berlin's oldest, and it's a little closer to the action, too. Prater Garten is right in the heart of Prenzlauer Berg and, though it's only open from May to September, it more than makes up for its winter absence by packing in the punters day after day in the warmer months. If you're hoping to meet friendly Berliners, or take a crowd of new friends for an affordable evening of boozing, then this is the place to do it.

Kastanienallee 7, Berlin

www.pratergarten.de

Bonanza Coffee Heroes, PRENZLAUER BERG

Berlin's drinking scene isn't only about alcohol – though, admittedly, boozing is a popular pursuit. Still, for non-drinkers, and those recovering from a night of excess, there's a growing cafe scene, led by the total coffee nerds at Bonanza. This was one of the first Berlin cafes to put a flat white on the menu, and after you've tried it you'll agree that the label 'heroes' is not hyperbole.

Oderberger Strasse 35, Berlin

www.bonanzacoffee.de

🚲 WHAT TO DO

There are plenty of very obvious attractions and landmarks in Berlin that you will find just by following your nose: the section of the Berlin Wall that makes up the East Side Gallery; Checkpoint Charlie; the various Jewish memorials and Nazi-era sites; the castle at Charlottenburg; the museums on Museum Island. And all of these places are interesting, and worth a visit. However, this is a city that rewards further digging, that reveals its character and heart to those who forgo the attractions and opt to wander, to poke around, talk to people and find their own way. The best thing about Berlin, too, is that it's a largely safe city that will welcome those travelling on their own.

Visit Tempelhof Airport

You want history? Tempelhof has history. This huge airfield and disused terminal was once used to test some of the world's first aeroplanes; it was then a base for the Nazis in the 1930s, housed prisoners in World War II, became an Allied headquarters post-war, and is now used as a refugee shelter, a filming location for major Hollywood movies, and a venue for open-air concerts and sporting competitions. You can do tours of the abandoned air terminal, which for travel nerds is absolute nirvana.

Platz der Luftbrücke 5, Berlin

www.thf-berlin.de

Sing at Bearpit Karaoke

If you're visiting Berlin in summer, this is an absolute must for a Sunday outing. First, you head down to the Mauerpark (probably via Bonanza Coffee), an open space in Prenzlauer Berg that sits below an old section of the wall, where a huge flea market takes place. Have a bit of a wander there, and then head over to the 'Bearpit', a small amphitheatre that plays host to one of Berlin's most enjoyable afternoon activities: open-air karaoke. Huge crowds turn up to cheer and sing along. Performers belt out the classics. As the fliers say: 'Showing off to strangers has never been easier'.

Mauerpark, Berlin

www.bearpitkaraoke.com

Top: The modern Spreebogen Park

Bottom: Buskers regularly perform at the Mauerpark in Prenzlauer Berg

Take an Alternative Berlin tour

Berlin is weird. It's arty. It's different. You'll figure this out very quickly. But you won't always know how to delve into the city's subcultures, how to access the stories and figures who make the city what it is. That's where Alternative Berlin comes in. The company's tour guides are all locally based artists and performers, active members of the city's street art, graffiti and underground scenes. They offer free walking tours of 'their' city, the alternative Berlin – it's a respectful and sustainable way to explore the city's artistic side.

www.alternativeberlin.com

Check out Teufelsberg

High up on a manmade hill in the Grunewald forest, in Berlin's west, sits Teufelsberg, a former US monitoring station: a spy base from which the Americans would listen in to Soviet communiqués during the occupation. These days the station is a dilapidated shell, a series of concrete platforms and domes covered in graffiti; however, on weekends a former US spy runs tours of the facility, and they're a fascinating insight into the way this city used to operate.

www.visitberlin.de/en/teufelsberg

LISBON

Lisbon is famous
for its classic tram
system, the best and
cheapest way to get
around the city

Lisbon is going places.

One look at the skyline confirms it: all of the cranes, the construction, the drilling and hammering. Any bad old days the Portuguese capital might have been through are over. Lisbon is booming. Now is the time to go.

There's such a feeling of optimism on the streets of Lisbon, such an air of positivity to the whole city that you can't help but be swept up in it. It seems like there's a celebration on here 24/7. Yes, Portugal had its problems: in the early 2000s the country was pretty much broke, its entire financial system in dire straits. But it has bounced back, and nowhere is that more evident than in buzzing, bustling Lisbon, the epicentre of all that's great and enjoyable about Portuguese life.

Lisbon is friendly; it's super-friendly. You'll have no problem meeting people here as a solo traveller. English is widely spoken by a youthful and vibrant population. There's a natural charm and sense of hospitality to most Portuguese, an easygoing manner that makes things simple for visitors to just slip into the Iberian lifestyle of good food and cheap wine, of art and music, of spending long afternoons somewhere nice with people you love.

The city itself, with its winding streets and many hills, at first makes no sense; it seems as if it will swallow you up and never spit you out. You hike up steep cobblestone streets, hoping for a viewpoint, hoping to figure out where you are, only to find more winding streets, more tile-clad buildings, more graffitied walls. Still, you shouldn't be worried about getting lost in Lisbon. If the streets are cobbled and winding then you're in the right place: in the older parts of town, in the areas that house the city's beating heart. This is good.

Lisbon is a city of neighbourhoods, each one distinct and worth dedicating a day to its exploration. There's Bairro Alto, on top of one of the city's seven hills, a hub of nightlife and cuisine, a bohemian spot that still has its share of old family-run stores amid the din. There's also Baixa, the downtown area filled with shops, set out on a welcome grid system. There's Alfama, perhaps the city's most charming district, with its narrow alleyways and tiled apartment blocks. There's trendy Príncipe Real, upmarket Belém, the Moorish-style Mouraria.

All of these areas have real character to them. Pavement cafes bubble with life. Kids kick footballs in small open squares. Each gap in the surrounding buildings provides a glimpse of something more, of the river that runs through the city, of laundry hanging from high windows, of the undulating sea of terracotta roofs that makes up greater Lisbon.

Solo travellers will have to look long and hard to find a better destination than the Portuguese capital. For starters, the city has some of the world's best hostels, places that have received award after award, with sharp design, modern facilities and a friendly atmosphere. They're indicative, too, of the overall experience of Lisbon, because they're also very affordable.

That's one of the greatest things about this place: for a major European city, Lisbon is very cheap. Food is cheap, particularly if you stick to the tascas, the casual eateries, and cervejarias, or pubs. Drink is also very affordable – you'll be hard pressed to find a glass of wine that costs more than €3. Mostly, wine (and beer) is around the €2 mark, and it's all local and extremely high quality. Everything, in fact, is affordable in Lisbon, from shops to attractions to public transport.

Lisbon has become something of a hub for backpackers in recent years, which makes meeting fellow travellers easy: you'll see them in the social areas of your hostel, on tours of the city, or even just propping up the bars around town. You can also tackle this city on your own: it's a largely safe place, with just the odd instance of petty theft to be wary of, and its eating and drinking scene is such that you won't feel awkward going out on your own. Order a few petiscos – the Portuguese form of tapas – and a glass of cheap wine and you're all set for a good evening.

There's really only one warning that needs to be applied to Lisbon, and it is: go there now. The city is becoming more popular by the day. Travellers are being drawn by its obvious charms, by its friendliness and affordability, its long history and exciting future. If you want to enjoy a place on the cusp of greatness, and harness all of that positivity and optimism, you need to get to Lisbon sooner rather than later. You won't regret it. ●

🚃 WHEN TO GO

Lisbon loves a festival. This city is almost always celebrating something, whether through music or dance or food or religious tradition. February is Carnaval time across Portugal, while June brings the Feast Day of St Anthony, a huge street-party-style event in Lisbon that's the perfect time to mix with the city's residents (and feast on grilled sardines); in November, São Martinho, once purely a religious celebration but now a festival of chestnuts and wine, is also a lot of fun. If, however, you're hoping to avoid the bulk of the crowds but still enjoy the city, the shoulder seasons (March–April and September–November) are beautiful.

Opposite: Alfama is one of Lisbon's oldest and most charming neighbourhoods

Top left: Pasteis de nata, the famed Portuguese tarts

Top right: Praca Rossio, one of Lisbon's many city squares

Bottom: Preserved seafood, a local specialty

Lisbon loves a festival. This city is almost always celebrating something.

WHERE TO STAY

Lisbon is home to an absolute embarrassment of high-quality, affordable hostels. Facilities such as rooftop terraces, swimming pools, beanbag rooms, foosball tables, and even – in one hostel – a freaking ball pit, are becoming standard issue in this city. The difficulty for me has been narrowing Lisbon's accommodation options down to just two. These are my personal favourites, no doubt, but if they're full when you visit you will very easily find an alternative.

One thing to bear in mind when booking a hostel in Lisbon is location, and whether it will suit the style of holiday you're planning. If you're hoping to access the city's nightlife scene, opt for Bairro Alto or Baixa. If you're up for more of a cultural stay, look to Belém. If it's an immersive and truly Lisbon experience you're chasing, then the winding streets of Alfama are for you.

Home Lisbon Hostel, BAIXA

This property was awarded 'best medium-sized hostel in the world' three years in a row by Hostelworld (in 2015, '16 and '17), and you can see why: it does everything right. It's got style – it's housed in a 200-year-old building in the Baixa neighbourhood, with classic old furnishings that look like they'd be better suited to a country manor than a hostel. It has excellent shared facilities, great social events such as pub crawls and walking tours, and it offers nightly 'Mamma's Dinners', which are shared meals cooked by the owner's mother.

Rua de São Nicolau 13, Lisbon

www.homelisbonhostel.com

Living Lounge Hostel, BAIXA

Homesick solo travellers: this is your new favourite hostel. Living Lounge is the perfect home away from home, an über-friendly boutique-style hostel in central Baixa. Each room here has been decorated by a local artist; the owners themselves are artists, and you can see the flair they've put into this property at every turn. The social areas are spacious and cool. The staff are helpful and kind. The nightly three-course dinners – which cost €9, including wine – are a godsend. Book this place. Now.

Rua do Crucifixo 116, Lisbon

www.livingloungehostel.com

Top left: Traditional tiles adorn the walls in Alfama

Top right: The Santa Justa elevator, open to the public, helps visitors scale the city's heights

Bottom right: Charm for days in the old city

Lisbon's best chefs
and providores
come together
under one roof
at the Time Out
Market

🍮 WHERE TO EAT

Portuguese food gets a bad rap. It's nowhere near as famous as, say, French
or Italian food. It's not even as well known as Spanish. If people know anything
about Portuguese cuisine it's that it's big on charcoal chicken and features a
certain sweet pastry. And, sure, those things are true. But there's so much more
to the food of Portugal than those two dishes, and you'll find out all about it
after a few days in Lisbon. Seafood here is a staple: there's a saying that the
Portuguese have more than 365 recipes for bacalhau, or salt cod – at least one
for each day of the year. They also make a mean sandwich, whether that's a
prego, a steak sandwich, or a bifana, a bread roll stuffed with pork. Food across
Lisbon is high quality, but it's also very affordable, meaning even solo travellers
on tight budgets will be able to eat out most nights.

Cervejaria Ramiro, INTENDENTE

For all you need to know about the greatness of Ramiro, look to the dessert course. Yes, the opening dishes will all be seafood, and they'll be some of the best seafood you've tasted: fat, juicy prawns grilled simply with salt; clams cooked in garlic and butter; langoustines boiled and served whole; oysters served fresh and tasty. But then you order the sobremesa, the dessert, which at Ramiro is a steak sandwich. A whole steak, in a roll. Now that's how you finish a meal in style.

Av. Almirante Reis 1, Lisbon

www.cervejariaramiro.pt

Time Out Market, CAIS DO SODRÉ

This should be tacky, and fairly average. A market run by a magazine? You don't have high hopes. And yet, if you were to eat in only one place during your entire stay in Lisbon, I would recommend the Time Out Market. The magazine house has repurposed a section of the old Mercado da Ribeira and turned it into a huge high-end food court, encouraging plenty of Lisbon's best chefs and most famous restaurants to open small, affordable outlets all under one roof. You can sample the full gamut of the city's best cuisine, right here.

Av. 24 de Julho, Lisbon

www.timeoutmarket.com

Pasteis de Belém, BELÉM

This place is no secret: Pasteis de Belém is the home of the pastel de nata, better known as the Portuguese tart, and it churns out some 23,000 of them every day, which explains the hungry hordes either waiting at the front counter or trying to find a seat in the cavernous interior at all times of the day. It's touristy, and it's packed. The thing is, though, it's also great. This bakery is the original and the best when it comes to pasteis de nata, and you'll find yourself ordering several.

Rua de Belém 84, Lisbon

www.pasteisdebelem.pt

Taberna da Rua das Flores, BAIRRO ALTO

One of the pleasures of Lisbon dining is the culture of petiscos, small plates similar to Spanish tapas. Taberna da Rua das Flores, a small, cosy eatery in Bairro Alto, does some of the best and most inventive petiscos in the city, with an ever-changing menu that takes its influences from classic Portuguese recipes, as well as flavours from around the world. The vibe here is classy, and it's a great spot for a quiet evening in your own company.

Rua das Flores 103, Lisbon

+351 21 347 9418

WHERE TO DRINK

There are plenty of people who visit Lisbon solely for the nightlife, for the traditional old pubs, cosy little drinking holes, rooftop bars and pumping clubs. This is a great city in which to go out and enjoy yourself, a lively place where the drinks are cheap and the crowds are friendly. If you're looking for casual bars filled with young, fun patrons who seem like they've called in from all parts of Europe, stick to Bairro Alto. For the more traditional, local side of life, Alfama is fantastic, while Príncipe Real has the cocktail bars if you're up for a fancy night out. It's no problem to go drinking solo in Lisbon – just pay attention to your security as you would in any city, and you should be in for a good night.

Tasca do Chico, ALFAMA

To feel the beating heart of Lisbon, you have to go to a fado bar and listen to this most traditional of local folk music. Fado is not a party starter, by any means: it's Portugal's answer to blues music, tales of lost love and sorrow woven through finger-picked guitar. It is, however, very popular, and a trip to an Alfama fado bar is a must. Tasca do Chico is one of the suburb's best, with live performances most nights.

Park Bar, BAIRRO ALTO

Being such a hilly city, Lisbon has its fair share of great views, and this is one of the best places to enjoy such vistas. Park Bar is perched on the top of a parking garage on the border of Bairro Alto and Príncipe Real, and as well as 180-degree views of the city, you'll also find a young crowd enjoying drinks and food amid an urban garden. This is a popular spot at sunset, but it also rages on late.

Rua dos Remedios 83, Lisbon

www.facebook.com/atasca.dochico

Calçada do Combro 58, Lisbon

www.facebook.com/parklisboaofficial

Quimera Brewpub, ALCÂNTARA

Portuguese wine is excellent, and the cocktails in this city are also pretty great. But sometimes you just want a beer, and this is the place to get it. Quimera does its own craft beer, served in an 18th-century tunnel in the middle of the Alcântara neighbourhood. This place is cosy and cool, and the beers make a pleasant change from the standard (and fairly beige) Portuguese fare.

Rua Prior do Crato 6, Lisbon

www.quimerabrewpub.pt

Pavilhão Chinês, PRÍNCIPE REAL

Going out drinking on your own? Worried you'll be bored? Head to Pavilhão Chinês, a classic old bar that has taken the more-is-more approach to interior decoration, lining its walls with more junk and collectables than you've ever seen: model planes, statues, uniforms, posters, mugs, action figurines ... Everything. Grab a drink and attempt to take it all in.

Rua Dom Pedro V 89, Lisbon

www.facebook.com/ pavilhaochineslisboa

Top: Portugal's most famous drink, port, for sale at a local store

Bottom: Streetside dining is always popular

WHAT TO DO

There's so much value in simply wandering Lisbon's streets to see whatever you see. The avenues themselves are attractions, often old cobbled paths lined with beautiful buildings, clad in traditional tiles, their ground floors taken up by little antique shops or cafes or bars or boutiques. You shouldn't feel you need a plan in Lisbon; it's fine to just spend the day wandering and exploring. If, however, you want to see sights, they are there. The riverfront suburb of Belém is home to the likes of the Mosteiro dos Jerónimos, a UNESCO-listed monastery, as well as Torre de Belém, a 16th-century fortified tower. There's a hilltop castle in Castelo and an art museum in Lapa. But, really, Lisbon is made for aimless exploring.

Ride the No. 28 tram

Alfama is the spot from which to begin another of Lisbon's great experiences, a ride on the No. 28 tram. This line is serviced by rattling turn-of-the-century carriages, which are attractions in themselves. The No. 28 actually begins down in Graça, before making its way through Alfama, into Baixa and Chiado, up through Bairro Alto and Príncipe Real, before terminating in Campo de Ourique. In other words, it's a whirlwind tour of the city's best sights, and it costs only a couple of euros.

Take a food tour

Once you've made it to Campo de Ourique, a fairly nondescript neighbourhood in Lisbon's west, don't just turn around and head home again. Instead, get to know one of the gastronomic hubs of the city. Taste of Lisboa runs food tours of Campo de Ourique, introducing visitors to plenty of traditional cuisine they would probably never have heard of before, as well as a great neighbourhood that's free of the tourist hordes.

www.tasteoflisboa.com

Visit Sintra

Though Lisbon itself is amazing, and will keep you occupied for weeks on end, it's worth making time to head out to the nearby town of Sintra, a UNESCO-listed site in the foothills of the Sintra Mountains. This was where Portugal's royal family used to spend their downtime, and the Palácio da Pena, a multicoloured castle on a hilltop, has got Instagram love written all over it.

Get lost in Alfama

This is an excellent place to begin your wanderings: Alfama, one of Lisbon's oldest districts. Once the domain of sailors and dock workers – the city's rough and ready – these days it's a slowly gentrifying though still character-filled neighbourhood of great little bars, cafes and shops. Don't miss the Sé Cathedral, and the viewpoints at Portas do Sol and the National Pantheon.

Top: Torre de Belem, a 16th-century fort on the Tagus River

Bottom: Alfama is ideal for aimless wandering

AMSTERDAM

A tourist stands
outside Amsterdam's
famous Rijksmuseum

Everyone knows **Amsterdam** – or at least, they *think* they know Amsterdam.

They know the sex-shop windows and the smoky coffee shops; the bucks party groups and boozy tour passengers; the heaving nightclubs and seedy backpacker bars. And that's fair. Amsterdam does have all of those things, and if you confine your visit to the city's most tourist-heavy parts, to Centrum and the Red Light District, with a brief detour to the Leidseplein for some magic mushrooms, then you too will be convinced that the city's attractions, its whole character, begin and end there.

But you'd be absolutely wrong. There's so much more to Amsterdam than the stuff everyone knows. That seedy side is worth experiencing, as it's something you'll probably never see anywhere else, but it's just the tiniest slice of the city, the side that most locals have nothing to do with; in fact, they barely even know it's there. True Amsterdam, the Amsterdam that will charm you and leave you wanting to come back for more, exists outside of its red-lit boundaries.

This is a city of green space, of huge parks and other reserves that change with the seasons, that morph from hugely popular hangout spots in the summer – venues for picnics and parties and everything in between – to quietly beautiful oases in winter, places for brisk walks or biking. The Vondelpark is one of Amsterdam's largest reserves, a huge area of trees and grass and ponds. Then there's sprawling Rembrandtpark, with its open spaces, and Sarphatipark, an urban playpen near the city's most popular market.

This is also a city of art, from old masters to the young and cutting-edge. Some of Europe's best museums and art galleries are in Amsterdam. This is a city of history, too, which you can't miss in the old storybook houses and cobbled lanes. There's much to be said for an aimless wander through areas such as the Jordaan and De Pijp, traditional neighbourhoods that these days are filled with shops selling antiques and modern bric-a-brac, vintage clothes and contemporary designs.

There's much to love about the drinking and dining scene in Amsterdam, too. Yes, there are mega-clubs here for the hard-partiers, and no shortage of seedy backpacker pubs, as well as infamous coffee shops like The Bulldog and The Grasshopper that peddle everything that's so notoriously legal in the 'Damage'. But that's not where locals go. Locals go to the 'brown cafes', traditional old drinking dens lined with brown wood panelling, where the food is tasty and the beer is great. They go to cool little bars on the streets of the Jordaan, or along the lanes of the Canal Ring.

This may sound as if there's a lot of ground to cover in Amsterdam, that you couldn't possibly expect to drop in for a few days and see all this stuff, but once again, you'd be in for a surprise. For a city with such a big reputation, Amsterdam is small. Fewer than 1 million people live here, and the place itself is very easy to cover in the same way all the locals do it, by bike. Hire one from a shop – there are loads – and you have your transport sorted. This is a bike-friendly city, safe and accessible, that's made for exploration on two wheels.

And just as Amsterdam is small, so is the Netherlands as a whole, meaning you can use this city as a base from which to explore the entire country. The quaint town of Haarlem is just a 15-minute train ride away. Utrecht, with its big student population and its canal-side drinking and dining scene, is 25 minutes away. The Hague is 45 minutes on the train; Rotterdam is an hour.

But there's enough in Amsterdam itself to keep you occupied, and you certainly won't feel alone as a solo traveller in this city. Though the Dutch can be a little stand-offish with strangers and aren't always easy to get to know straightaway, there's such a large tourism industry here that you're never short of people to share your experience with. Some you'll meet will be fellow short-term travellers; others will be in Amsterdam for the long haul. Regardless, it's easy to find company here.

And even if you don't, or you choose not to, Amsterdam is a safe city that's simple enough to navigate and enjoy on your own. It's easy to wander museums on your own, to shop on your own, to pull up a stool at a brown cafe on your own, and to jump on a bike and make your way around the city on your own.

Leave plenty of time for your visit to Amsterdam. You might be drawn in by all of the touristy clichés – and they can be enjoyable – but it's the local secrets that will make you stay. ●

Leave plenty of time for
your visit to Amsterdam.

Opposite: Inside the famed Rijksmuseum

Top left: The Nemo Science Museum

Top right: Wooden tulips on sale

Bottom: There's no better – or more popular – way to get around Amsterdam than on a bike

 WHEN TO GO

As unlikely as it sounds, given the greatness of the European summer, April is the best month to be in Amsterdam. The biggest event on the Netherlands' calendar, King's Day, takes place on 27 April, and the city goes absolutely crazy for it. If you want to see the Dutch at their best, this is the time to visit. April is also the time for the annual Tulip Festival, and it's the month with the least rain. Plus, the tourist crush isn't too hectic. In mid-summer Amsterdam is busy and expensive; still, the Gay Pride Parade, in late July and early August, is worth being in town for.

Top left: A busker entertains the crowd at Dam Square

Top right: Amsterdam's charming streets

Bottom: The city's famous canals are ripe for exploration

WHERE TO STAY

There's a downside to Amsterdam: it's not cheap. You can expect to pay €30 or even more for a bed in a hostel dorm, and far more for a private room. Amsterdam is small and it's popular, which means real estate is pricey. That's just how it is, unfortunately. On the upside, the city's popularity with backpackers means there are a lot of hostels set up to appeal to that market, and if you book ahead you should have no problems securing a bed in a friendly, clean and sociable hostel that's close to the action. (Be warned, however, that if a hostel here claims to be a 'party hostel', then it will not be kidding.)

When picturing Amsterdam, think of a set of concentric semicircular rings: these are the famous canals, and they fan out from Centrum, the central district (where you'll also find the Red Light District). The bulk of Amsterdam's hostels are here, with a few scattered along the canals. If you're looking for a slightly cheaper stay, but still in striking distance of Centrum, look around the Vondelpark, or in Amsterdam Noord.

ClinkNOORD, AMSTERDAM NOORD

This is the place to stay when you want to be in Central Amsterdam, but you don't actually want to be in Central Amsterdam. ClinkNOORD is located just across the IJ River, a short ferry ride from Centraal station. The property is an old 1920s laboratory that has been refurbed into a smart hostel, which has a library and work space, a cafe and a bar, and dorms of various sizes (including women-only dorms) with all of the mod cons. This is the perfect place to chill out with like-minded solo travellers when you get tired of the Amsterdam craziness.

Badhuiskade 3, Amsterdam

www.clinkhostels.com

Flying Pig, CENTRUM

If it's the classic hard-partying Amsterdam experience you're chasing, then these two hostels – one downtown, one uptown – are for you. The Flying Pig is notorious, in good ways and bad. Both properties are clean and friendly, with modern facilities, and both are in great locations. They also have bars that are open until 3am with local DJs and daily drinks specials, 'smoking rooms' with beanbags and lounge pillows, plus 'munchy food' for sale. Great if that's what you're after; not if you're not.

Nieuwendijk 100, Amsterdam
Vossiusstraat 46, Amsterdam

www.flyingpig.nl

 WHERE TO EAT

Amsterdam has never been known as a culinary destination. Local Dutch food is mostly quite uninspiring, and international food here has tended to range from authentic and tasty to cheap and nasty. However, things are changing, rapidly. The city's old standard eateries are being forced to lift their game by a new wave of chefs breathing life into traditional recipes, and tinkering with different styles of food. Though the city's better restaurants come with high price tags, there are plenty of options for travellers on a budget to access delicious cuisine, with casual eateries spread across the city. Solo diners are rare at the more expensive restaurants, but no one will bat an eye at the following places.

Top: Traditional Dutch cheeses ripening

Bottom: Amsterdam's improving food scene means a wider selection of international cuisine

Febo, VARIOUS LOCATIONS

'De lekkerste', proclaims Febo's slogan, meaning 'the tastiest', and come 3am on any given night in Amsterdam you'll be inclined to agree. Febo serves the city's best and most authentic Dutch fast food, the likes of meat-stuffed croquettes and 'bitterballen', deep-fried balls of meaty sauce dipped in mustard. These treats are served in tiny, vending machine–style windows that don't require human interaction. There are Febo outlets across the city.

www.febo.nl

Vlaams Friteshuis Vleminckx, CENTRUM

Put a Dutch person and a Belgian in the same room and ask who makes the world's best fried potatoes and you'll have a brawl on your hands. The truth is that despite Belgium's being more famous, there's no loser: they're both great. To sample some of the finest fries in the Netherlands (served in a paper cone, slathered in rich mayonnaise), head to Vleminckx, an eternally busy friteshuis, or chip house, in central Amsterdam.

Voetboogstraat 33, Amsterdam

www.vleminckxdesausmeester.nl

Albert Cuyp Market, DE PIJP

There's a lot to love about Albert Cuyp, a large market that takes place six days a week on the streets of De Pijp. There's good fresh produce here, perfect for picking up a few eats to cook in the hostel. You can also sample some Dutch favourites, including pickled herring with onion (better than it sounds), and stroopwafels – thin waffles sandwiched around caramel syrup (as good as it sounds). There are also loads of great restaurants and bars around the market area.

Albert Cuypstraat, Amsterdam

www.albertcuyp-markt.amsterdam

Winkel 43, JORDAAN

Here's another local treat you have to get your hands on: appeltaart, or Dutch apple pie. Done properly, it's served as a huge slice, with big hunks of apple stewed with spices wrapped in short-crust pastry and topped with fresh whipped cream – and Winkel 43, a bustling shop in the Jordaan, does it properly. During summer, grab a seat at a communal table in the sun and feast.

Noodermarkt 43, Amsterdam

www.winkel43.nl

WHERE TO DRINK

There are several sides to the Amsterdam drinking and nightlife scene. There's the old-school local scene, which consists of quiet beers, small plates of food and good conversation. There's the new-school local scene, which ranges from cocktail bars to craft beer pubs to open-air, riverside playgrounds. There's the seedy nightlife scene, based around the Red Light District: the strip clubs and sex shows, the coffee shops peddling legal weed, the tourist pubs selling overpriced beer. There's the backpacker scene, which involves copious consumption in hostels and dive bars across the city centre. And finally there's the party scene, where people from all the previous locations congregate in sweaty clubs to dance into the small hours.

Brouwerij't IJ, AMSTERDAM OOST

This craft brewery has been in business a little over thirty years, though you'll think it's a lot older thanks to the charming old building it's housed in, beneath Amsterdam's tallest windmill. This is the place to head on a warm, sunny afternoon, to relax in the canal-side beer garden, mix with people of all ages and nationalities, drink great beer and just enjoy Europe at its finest.

Funenkade 7, Amsterdam

www.brouwerijhetij.nl

Café Chris, JORDAAN

For the ultimate hit of legit Dutch drinking culture, head to a brown cafe, one of the traditional Dutch pubs named for their wood-panelled walls. You'll find brown cafes spread across the city: they're all old and a little daggy, the beer is cheap, the snacks are tasty, and the crowd pleasant. Café Chris is one of the originals, a bar that opened in 1624 and has been serving the thirsty masses ever since.

Bloemstraat 42, Amsterdam

www.cafechris.nl

> In winter the Amsterdammers tend to hibernate; in summer, however, everyone comes out to play.

A classic "brown cafe"

Amsterdam Roest, CENTRUM

In winter the Amsterdammers tend to hibernate; in summer, however, everyone comes out to play, and on a good day you'll find people pulling all of their lounge-room furniture onto the street to sunbake, or picnicking in parks, or heading to one of Amsterdam's many beer gardens or open-air bars. Roest is one of the best of the latter establishments, a sprawling canal-side space with an artificial beach and an adult-sized jungle gym. Oh, and beer.

Jacob Bontiusplaats 1, Amsterdam

www.amsterdamroest.nl

Club NYX, CENTRUM

You could choose any number of great clubs in which to spend a long evening in Amsterdam, but NYX is surely this open-minded city's best representative: a divey, three-floor establishment where anything goes. NYX is ostensibly a gay club, though you'll find everyone is welcome, and it makes a pleasant change from the beer-chugging, shot-slugging backpacker bars.

Reguliersdwarsstraat 42, Amsterdam

www.clubnyx.nl

WHAT TO DO

Most visitors' first daytime activity in Amsterdam is sleeping off a hangover. And that's fine – it's that sort of city. But it is worth attempting to actually leave the hostel in the daylight hours to explore this place, because it has a lot to offer. Amsterdam is very easy to navigate, once you have a bike, and small enough to cover the highlights in only a few short days. You can repent all of your night-time sins during the day here, taking in high culture at the museums, shopping for fresh food in the markets, checking out local boutiques and other interesting stores, or taking a ferry across the IJ River to check out the underrated Noord district. Alternatively, you could just call past a coffee shop and get legally stoned. Decisions, decisions ...

Visit a coffee shop

You're in Amsterdam – you should definitely check out a coffee shop (remember, somewhat confusingly in this city, cafes sell coffee, and coffee shops sell marijuana). Even if you don't want to smoke, a quick whip through a coffee shop is an educational experience. Some of the city's best, and those not tailored entirely for tourists, include Tweede Kamer (www.tweedekamer.shop), and La Tertulia (www.coffeeshoptertulia.com). Though it may seem that anything goes in Amsterdam, it's still illegal to smoke pot in public places, so consume it in the coffee shop or stay in a smoke-friendly hostel.

Hit the markets

For a slightly more wholesome experience, check out Amsterdam's many markets, where you'll have the chance to mix with locals going about their daily business. The city's markets are often centuries old, and offer everything from fruits and vegetables to vintage vinyl records. Some of the best include the Waterlooplein market for vintage clothes and antiques, the Bloemenmarkt for Dutch flowers, the Noordermarkt for farm-fresh food, and the Nieuwmarkt for cheese. Opening days and hours vary with the seasons, so check before visiting.

www.iamsterdam.com

Hire a bike

This. Every visitor to Amsterdam should do this. The city is built for biking, with dedicated lanes everywhere you go, as well as a culture of respect for those getting around on two wheels. Every solo traveller should have a bike: it's your ticket to seeing Amsterdam cheaply, authentically and enjoyably. If you're not super-confident aboard a pedal-powered steed, maybe start off with a guided bike tour, which will help you get to know the city and its cycling customs. Mike's Bikes runs some great tours, and you'll be able to rent one of their bikes for your whole stay.

www.mikesbiketoursamsterdam.com

Tour the museums

In some cities you'd be wasting your time hanging out in museums and art galleries all day, but Amsterdam is not one of them. Plenty of the world's finest works can be seen here, and it'd be a crime to give them a miss. Begin in the excellent Van Gogh Museum for a full run-down of the famed Dutchman's works, before moving on to the huge Rijksmuseum, the Rembrandt House Museum, the Amsterdam Museum and the Anne Frank House.

www.iamsterdam.com

Top: A bike is the ideal mode of transport

Bottom: Spend some time touring Amsterdam's museums, including the Rijksmuseum

CHAPTER EIGHT

YOU'RE GOING WHERE?

Opposite top: A neon cowboy in Las Vegas, USA

Opposite bottom: A view of Taormina, Italy

Top left: The Pyramids of Giza, Egypt

Bottom left: All-in in Vegas

Bottom middle: The stunning islands off East New Britain, Papua New Guinea

Bottom right: Mountain flowers in Taormina, Italy

Thump. Thump. Thump.

The neighbours are at it again, rattling the ornaments on my dresser. *Thump. Thump. Thump.* At this time of night, the rhythmic banging on the adjoining wall can only be due to one thing.

They're honeymooners, so it's understandable. They're in Tahiti, too, a romantic place of swaying palms and a gentle sun, so it makes even more sense. But, still. Spare the single travellers for at least one night.

Trouble is, this is just the beginning. Next day I board a flight to one of the outer islands of French Polynesia, and catch the music being piped through the plane's stereo system. As we taxi to the runway, the chorus kicks in: 'I only have eyes for you.' You've got to be kidding me.

Solo travel is a blast, but it's a lot more of a blast when you're not stuck on a tropical island surrounded by honeymooners, canoodling and staring quizzically at 'That Single Guy'. After all, a long walk on the beach is improved immeasurably by having someone to walk next to you. And there's something wholly disheartening about drinking a fruity cocktail by yourself.

But anyway, back to honeymooner heaven. The island of Moorea, only a short boat ride from Tahiti, is basically shaped like a heart, so you can take that as fair warning.

At the ferry terminal I'm greeted by an enormous Polynesian guy who swings my backpack onto his shoulder like it's a handbag and looks around behind me.

'How many more?' he asks.

'Um ... none.'

He looks shocked. 'Just you? By yourself?'

I nod and he shrugs, tosses my bag into the back of the van and jumps into the driver's seat. As he guns the engine and pulls out onto the road, he fixes me with a look in the rear-view mirror.

'No wife?' he asks.

I sigh. 'No wife.'

He shrugs again and off we go.

After a few hours on the island I can see why he was so surprised. Like some sort of Noah's Ark of romance, everyone on Moorea travels in twos (for similar reproductive purposes). And when they're not making the walls shake in their luxury resorts, the honeymooners invade the local activities. I'm soon on a quad-biking trip through the island's volcanic centre and the joy begins as we're signing the indemnity forms.

'Just put your passenger's name in the space here, please,' says the guide, Manu, pointing at the sheet of paper.

> Like some sort of Noah's Ark of romance, everyone on Moorea travels in twos.

'Ah ... I don't have a passenger.'

'No passenger?' Manu purses his lips. 'Okay.'

Off we go, six new husbands driving their six new wives – and me, trundling along at the back. The empty seat behind me is a silent reminder of the unwritten rule being broken. Soon, Manu has stopped everyone to explain the Polynesian custom of wearing a flower behind your left ear to show people you're spoken for. 'But if a girl was single,' Manu continues, 'and she saw a single man – maybe you, Ben, because you are on your own – then she would wear the flower in her right ear.'

'Thanks, Manu.'

We're about to set off again, except the Italians on the bike in front of me are trying to kiss wearing their helmets, resulting in minimal lip contact and an awkward clashing of plastic visors. As everyone looks on with an aw-isn't-that-sweet gaze,

the two manage to manoeuvre their heads into the right position to lock lips. Groan.

What's up next? Jam tasting! Manu takes us to a little factory where tasting plates are handed out. 'And remember,' Manu says, 'it's one plate per couple.' After a moment, his eyes land on me. 'Oh, Ben, you can have one for yourself.'

We motor along on our merry way, the couples all pausing for the occasional kiss (the French husband earns a punch in the shoulder for taking a river at speed and soaking his beloved). I fly solo at the back. Eventually, as the day winds down, I find a practical use for my status as That Single Guy. At a lookout with a view all the way back to Tahiti, the Italian newlyweds cautiously approach me.

'Excuse me,' the guy says politely, proffering his camera. 'Could you make a photo of us please?' •

This chapter, as with my recommendations of where *to go*, should come with a caveat.

There's nowhere you can't travel by yourself if you really want to go. If you're dying to lounge around by a resort pool with a cocktail in your hand and you have no one who wants to join you in such an endeavour, then by all means go by yourself. If you've always wanted to visit somewhere that's considered dangerous and are prepared to take your chances, then with the right planning and precautions you should be able to visit solo.

The following cities and countries aren't iron-clad no-go zones for single travellers. My point is more that, just as there are some destinations that lend themselves particularly well to solo travel, there are others that might be best avoided or saved for when you have company. You'll get to these places at some point, and you'll be with a partner or a group of friends and have the time of your life. For now, though, maybe plan to go somewhere else.

Top: The Vegas Strip by night – a good place to have a partner in crime

Bottom: A fisherman hopes for a catch near Rabaul, Papua New Guinea

LAS VEGAS, USA

It's the strangest feeling: waking up in Vegas without a hangover. It's 9am and I'm up and I'm alive; I'm wandering out into the blinding glare of the desert sun, strolling past the hotel pool and finding it empty, the swim-up bar and Jacuzzi bare, and I half expect to see tumbleweed rolling past and find out I'm in *The Walking Dead*. Nothing much happens in the morning on the Vegas Strip, because no one is around. They're all sleeping off their bad decisions from the night before, or waking up and swearing that they definitely, probably, hopefully won't do it all again tonight.

And yet, I'm not. I'm not because I barely even had a drink the night before, because I'm here on my own. Vegas solo: it's a strange feeling, like turning up to a party full of people you don't know. You don't instantly dive into the celebration. You stand back a little bit, take it all in, leave time to ponder the city's ridiculousness.

I've been to Las Vegas before and done it properly. I came here on the ultimate cliché, the bucks, or bachelor, party. I was here with a group of mates and we legitimately lost one of our friends. We last saw him at a club at four in the morning and when the time came to leave the city and fly out to the wedding the next day we just couldn't find him. We made contact a few hours later, when our plane had landed. He sent us a text that said only, 'Viva Las Vegas.'

So, yeah, I've seen the crazy side of Vegas, the party side, the classic side that the city is so famous for. And now I'm back here on my own, and it's weird. Last night I went to a show, I wandered the Strip, I watched people gamble, then I went to bed. By midnight. It's unheard of.

The thing is, Vegas is a city that deserves company. It's a party city. It's a place people come to in groups to go wild. It's safe for solo travellers, undoubtedly. But of all the times I've been here, I've enjoyed myself a lot more with friends. Gambling on your own isn't fun; it's sad. Doing karaoke in some seedy bar also feels a little weird without a support crew. Going out to clubs, going on roller-coasters, drinking neon drinks out of plastic yard glasses, going to pool parties or places you know you'll regret – they are all more fun with friends. I'd leave Vegas until you can visit with a few of them.

> To put it bluntly, travelling in Cairo is not easy.

Top left: The chaotic streets of central Cairo, Egypt

Top right: Khan al-Khalili Bazaar in Cairo, one of the world's great marketplaces

Bottom right: An ablution fountain at Cairo's Al-Sultan Barquq mosque

CAIRO, EGYPT

My taxi driver has no idea where the airport is. Seriously, this is not a scam. We've agreed on a price and there is no meter – he's not driving around in circles in some attempt to get more money out of me. He's driving around in circles because he has no idea where he's going, or where the airport is.

At first I thought it was a communication breakdown. I'd hailed this clapped-out old cab at random, from the street, thrown my pack in the back and climbed in. I said I wanted to go to the airport, we settled on a fare and then off we went, careening into the insane Cairo traffic, tearing around at great speed, heading, I thought, to the airport.

But then we stopped at a light and the driver turned to me and said something in Arabic that made it clear he didn't know where we were going. I flapped my arms around, made like a plane taking off. 'Airport?'

The driver grunted, gunned the engine, flew back into the maelstrom.

Now he's still driving fast, but he's obviously not sure where. He's talking to other cab drivers who pull up next to him, yelling in rapid-fire Arabic. Those drivers are looking at me in the back seat, I'm doing my arm-flapping

routine, we're driving again for another few minutes and then repeating the whole process with another driver. How is it that no one in this city knows how to get to the airport?

And yet, this is Cairo. Cairo is big and intimidating. It's chaotic. It's ramshackle. It's in your face. It's the kind of place where things don't always go the way you assume they will, where something as simple as catching a taxi to the airport can become a high-stress activity. To put it bluntly, travelling in Cairo is not easy. This is particularly true if you're alone, and even more so if you're a woman. Solo female travellers quickly become a focus of attention in Cairo, attention that's not always welcome. You can expect catcalling, whistling, sometimes worse. You might not be in any real danger, but the intimidation factor will be high here. It's not somewhere you're likely to feel comfortable.

That doesn't mean that solo travellers of any gender can't visit Cairo. There's a lot to love about this city, and plenty of well-meaning, friendly locals happy to help you out. If you're after comfort, though, and ease of movement, and even peace of mind, I would leave this one until you have company – and a driver who knows where the airport is.

TAORMINA, ITALY

There's a couple smooching on the balcony. Actually, scratch that – there are about 20 couples smooching on the balcony. They're all lined up like football players at national anthem time, with other couples behind them, patiently waiting for the frontrunners to finish locking lips so they can dive into position at the edge of the balcony and play some tonsil tennis of their own.

It's sunset, which is prime smooching time at any location. Some of the couples here are being professionally photographed in this intimate moment, while others take iPhone selfies to immediately post on Instagram and wait for the envy to arrive, while a few more are settling for simply burning the moment into their memories.

The place is Taormina, a mountain town on the eastern coast of Sicily. The balcony is part of the town's main square, a spectacular spot that opens out to views of the Mediterranean, the Sicilian coastline, a perpetually smoking Mount Etna and the slowly setting sun. This might just be one of the most romantic places in the world, a fact that's rammed home to anyone who might have been strangely unaware by all of the couples celebrating their couple-ness on the streets and lanes and balconies and restaurants of this lovely little town. A little kiss here, a bit of hand-holding

there. The weather is warm and the nights are long. It's perfect.

The only problem with all this love and lust is when you're travelling here alone. I'm the weird guy walking around on his own, drinking wine bought by the glass, taking solo selfies at spectacular locations and slurping strands of spaghetti without the benefit of someone attached to the other end. Taormina is unbelievably beautiful. However, given its status as a romance capital, and its population of those who wish to be romantic, it's maybe not ideal for solo travellers.

There is respite here if you really want to visit. There's Hostel Taormina, this expensive holiday town's sole provider of budget accommodation and a home away from home for the 25 or so travellers who squeeze in each night. Everyone there is in the same situation. If they'd visited Taormina with a partner, they wouldn't be staying in a dorm.

Still, Taormina isn't a party kind of place – it's a hand-holding-over-candlelit-dinner kind of place. It's a staring-into-someone's-eyes place. It's a getting-down-on-one-knee place. I'd leave it until you have someone to join you.

> I've seen things in this amazing nation that I never even believed existed.

"

A Hulu tribesman displays his traditional adornments

PAPUA NEW GUINEA

There are more than 7 million people living in Papua New Guinea, who hail from more than 7000 different cultural groups and speak over 800 different languages. Is it any wonder there are problems in this country? Is anyone really surprised at the odd outbreak of violence? Some countries with two cultural groups struggle to keep a lid on things. Try having 7000.

Of course, there's more to PNG than tribal conflict. Those 7000 cultural groups also serve to produce one of the most diverse and interesting adventure travel destinations on the planet, where every town is a new country. I've seen things in this amazing nation that I never even believed existed. I've been to a Baining fire dance, a ceremony up in the mountains near Rabaul that involves men in huge masks emerging from a pitch-dark forest to leap through the flames of and dance on a bonfire. I've hung out with traditional boat-makers at the Kenu and Kundu Festival in Alotau and done some of the best scuba-diving of my life in PNG.

I've done all of this, however, with company: finding safety in numbers. Papua New Guinea is an incredible place, but it's also unpredictable and sometimes dangerous. Go there with people who know what they're doing, who know the signs that something is up and the places to avoid. You should definitely visit PNG. Just maybe not on your own.

CHAPTER NINE

FIVE AMAZING JOURNEYS

That might be a cliché, but it's also true. The glory of travel is not only in being somewhere, but in getting there. It's in all of the adventures that moving from one place to another entails. It's in taking your time and exploring the bits that connect the dots in this world, the little towns and the big open spaces that you never knew existed. A great journey opens you up to so many possibilities, to a million forks in the road that each offer something new.

I love to make travel a journey, to set a beginning and an end and just allow the rest to shape itself, for the highlights and the lowlights to reveal themselves as time, and I, go on. This is travel in its purest form, enthralling and unexpected. Movement is excitement. Every day is something new.

Of course, some journeys are better suited to solo travellers than others. These journeys offer the perfect balance of adventure and safety, the opportunity to meet people or to strike out on your own if you so desire. The following are five trips I've taken solo that I've absolutely loved, and would recommend to any traveller who is hoping to embrace the beauty of the journey. •

Opposite top: Hikers take a break on the Salkantay Trail, Peru

Top: The plains of the Masai Mara in Kenya

Bottom: Up close and personal in Hanoi, Vietnam

NAIROBI TO CAPE TOWN

There are plenty of opportunities for elephant spotting in Etosha National Park, Namibia

Africa gets into your blood.
It seeps into your bones.

It lodges itself somewhere deep within you and never lets go. There's something about the silent beauty of an African dawn: the savannah slowly coming into focus, the anticipation building. There's something about those fiery dusks, too, about a huge sun framed by halos of dust kicked up by a million hooves. There are the rituals you slip into on an African journey: the campfire meals, the sunset G&Ts, the endless repetition of songs by Paul Simon and Toto.

Nowhere else in the world provides such a thrilling travel experience as the African continent, such a wild adventure, such a feeling of connection to the natural world. This vast area is ideal for long explorations that move from country to country, working your way through all of the different cultures, the different cities and moods.

My first trip to Africa was a journey from Nairobi, in Kenya, down to Cape Town, in South Africa, and it's one I've never forgotten. It took more than three months: three months of staying in rough campsites, sleeping on hard ground, cooking my own food over an open fire and packing up every day to move on. By the time I got to the end and saw Table Mountain lurking on the horizon, I was more than ready to turn around and do the whole thing all over again.

This East African journey is the perfect introduction to the continent, a way to appreciate so many of its countries and places, with the backing of good tourist infrastructure, decent roads and relative safety. It's also ideal for solo travellers, as you'll inevitably join a group here and make friends as you go, companions that you'll get to know better than anyone you've ever met through this shared adventure.

You'll explore some of the world's most famous game parks on this trip, waiting in hope to see the 'Big 5': lions, leopards, elephants, buffalos, rhinos. You'll feel the buzz of African cities, their joy and unpredictability. You'll work your way out of trouble, maybe changing tyres, maybe digging out wheels, maybe just searching through a supermarket to figure out what's good to eat.

Your life will change with this journey. You'll have experiences and you'll meet people you will never forget. Africa will get into your blood, and you'll never be the same again. •

THE HIGHLIGHTS

There are so many highlights on the road from Nairobi to Cape Town that you'll lose count. The safest and easier path goes through Kenya, Tanzania, Malawi, Zambia, Botswana, Namibia and South Africa; it will feature visits to the Serengeti, the Masai Mara National Park, the Okavango Delta and the Etosha National Park, and will call through Zanzibar, Lake Malawi, Victoria Falls and Stellenbosch; it will include cities, towns, villages and campsites in the middle of nowhere.

Game viewing, obviously, is a major highlight of this trip. Seeing lions, elephants, leopards, cheetahs and about a thousand exotic animal species you've never even heard of, in the flesh, is seriously exciting. And then there's the semi-autonomous island nation of Zanzibar, where you can hang out on the white-sand beaches or explore the history of Stone Town. Riding in a dug-out canoe in the Okavango Delta is a unique thrill. Seeing Victoria Falls, 'the smoke that thunders', is something you'll never forget. Touring the wineries of Stellenbosch in South Africa is a welcome change of pace. In fact, even just an average driving day in Africa, watching as the world rattles by through an open window, will be one of the greatest experiences of your life.

Top: Botswana's local San people

Bottom: Deadvlei, a spectacular part of the Namib-Naukluft National Park in Namibia

Top: Diners at Giraffe Manor, a boutique hotel and sanctuary in Nairobi, where the giraffes join guests for breakfast

Bottom: An ostrich family hits the road in Meru National Park, Kenya

THE DANGERS

The countries of East and Southern Africa are edgy, unpredictable destinations, which means things might — and, in fact, probably will — go wrong on your journey through them. Some of these dramas are unavoidable and often just a case of being in the wrong place at the wrong time. Others, meanwhile, can be easily mitigated. Ensure you're up to date on vaccinations before taking this trip, and stock up on anti-malarial medication. Get good travel insurance with full medical and evacuation cover. Make sure you have several methods of accessing money, stored in different places. Don't go out at night alone; rather, take a group of fellow travellers. Obey your guides' instructions in game parks. And check your government's travel warnings for the latest safety information.

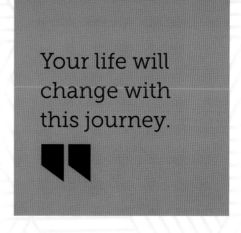

Your life will
change with
this journey.

THE TRAVEL PLAN

You could tackle this journey without doing an organised tour. It's possible to use public transport in East Africa, to ride matatus, the shared taxis, and local buses, but I wouldn't recommend it, particularly if you're travelling in Africa for the first time, and doing it alone. By far the easier and safer option is to join an 'overlander', one of the many truck tours that traverse the continent, guiding travellers through the highlights and steering them clear of any potential pitfalls.

You'll notice I said truck tours, not bus tours. In Africa the vehicles you ride in aren't luxury coaches, they're big rigs, modified trucks that have four-wheel drive and plenty of space for passengers, tents and luggage. On board you have a driver, a trip leader and maybe a cook. You also have safety in numbers, fellow passengers to share your African adventure with and make potentially problematic things like

going out at night in a city, as well as navigating this sometimes intimidating continent, a lot easier.

There are plenty of companies that run overland tours from Nairobi to Cape Town, with many different styles and pricepoints. The best include Acacia Africa, Intrepid Travel, G Adventures and Oasis Overland.

THE TIMING

If you're planning to do the full Nairobi to Cape Town journey, you'll need to allow about three months. However, this trip can be broken down into smaller chunks, with itineraries available through the overland companies that can be as little as ten days long. Winter is the best time of year to go, when the skies are clear and water sources in the game parks are scarce – making wildlife easier to find – and the wildebeest migration is running through Kenya and Tanzania. That means travelling between June and September.

ANTARCTICA

An expedition vessel
visible from the
Antarctic shoreline

'The sailors have a message for everyone,' said **Rodrigo**, keeping his voice conspiratorially low.

'There's going to be a party tonight. Down on the sailors' deck after dinner. They have drinks and music.'

This was kind of a surprise. Officially, the sailors' deck didn't exist for us passengers. It was the place where all of the dirty, behind-the-scenes work was done, where the ship was maintained and the services were carried out to keep everything on the passenger decks above running as smoothly as possible.

The sailors weren't allowed in our zone, and we hadn't even been told what was below. But a message had been passed to one of the Spanish-speaking passengers, Rodrigo, and tonight we were invited to cross the threshold.

This was day 10 of an 11-day journey, a trip from the southern Argentinian city of Ushuaia to Antarctica aboard an 80-passenger expedition vessel. Those passengers were a mixed bunch, from retiree couples to a fairly ragtag group of young backpackers taking advantage of one of the cheaper cruise lines doing a discounted final trip for the season.

We'd all spent the past nine days acting in the way most visitors to Antarctica act: seriously. We'd attended lectures on biology and geology during the journey down to the continent. We'd watched breathlessly as thousands of penguins lived their funny, wobbly lives around us when we finally made landfall. We'd even kept a lid on things when we visited a Ukrainian research station and were encouraged to drink the scientists' homemade vodka and beat them at pool.

But now we'd left Antarctica, and things had changed. There was an air of celebration, a feeling of achievement, a need to revert to regular travelling behaviour, and the expedition crew were about to provide an outlet.

Down on the sailors' deck, after dinner. Word got around, from the Dutch couple to the German girls to the Spanish students to the group of Aussie mates. It was on. Who knew cruising could be so fun? I'd always pictured it as an activity for the older generations, one that offered shuffleboard and buffets to pillage. But this? I loved every minute of this. I loved the feeling of casting out to

sea, headed due south. I loved the lectures, the mess dinners, the penguin encounters, the research base visits, the infinite sunsets and the party atmosphere on the way home. It matched me perfectly: part adventure, part education, part celebration.

And still, it wasn't over.

That night, we all finished our dinner, gave each other knowing looks, and then headed towards the back of the boat to get below decks. Down there, the Argentinian crew had laid out a few bottles of booze, set up cheap disco lights, and cranked up the music. There was soon drinking, and dancing, and the fairly obvious realisation that the crew's intention in throwing this shindig was mainly to pick up the single female passengers – something they had some success in. For the rest of us it was just a long, fun night in a part of the ship we weren't supposed to be in, letting off steam after ten days of being good. It's not a highlight you expect from a cruise in Antarctica – but it's one you might just get. •

Top: Cruise passengers make landfall in Antarctica

Bottom: Penguins provide endless entertainment

Top: The incredible
stillness of Antarctica

Bottom left: How far from
home? Signpost at the
Ukrainian Research Station
in Antarctica

Bottom right: A colony
of gentoo penguins

THE HIGHLIGHTS

Antarctica is amazing. It's another world. It's cold and stark and brooding, a place where danger lurks in the air, where the weather can just turn and everything goes bad. But it's also surprisingly warming, the sort of place that fills you with joy at the sight of penguins tottering around in their big groups, or seals lazing about on icebergs, or just all that white-clad natural beauty. Even the experience of getting there, of being there, of coming back – all this is an attraction, a cherished memory.

Antarctica can only be accessed via an expedition cruise, and it's the trip of a lifetime, from start to finish. It's the long days at sea, days that can turn rough and nasty. It's your first sight of the great southern continent, the tips of the snow-covered hills appearing on the horizon. It's all the interactions with wildlife, the rides in rubber dinghies through iceberg fields, up to deserted beaches. It's the people, too, those you meet on board, the fellow adventurers who turn into new best friends.

THE DANGERS

The main danger of this journey is the same for solo travellers as for everyone else: seasickness. The Drake Passage – the body of water that separates the southern tip of Argentina from the northernmost point of Antarctica – is notoriously unpredictable, with a tendency towards violence. We're talking regular swells of between 10

and 12 metres (30 and 40 feet), with anything up to 20 metres (65 feet – that's a wave the size of a six-storey building) liable to hit. Even if you don't usually get seasick, there is a chance you will in the Drake Passage. Once you're through there, however, it's literally plain sailing, with the only worry being the right clothes to combat the cold. Bring plenty of layers.

THE TRAVEL PLAN

Most expedition cruises leave from Ushuaia in southern Argentina. Though a trip like this might seem out of reach for the budget traveller, there are ways to make the dream come true for a reasonable amount of money. To begin with, choose to travel at the start or the end of the season, when discounts will be offered. At the end of the season, it's also possible to arrive in Ushuaia without a booking and negotiate a cut-price fare. That is a little risky, though. You can also opt to share a triple cabin, rather than a double, to bring prices down. The Australian-based company Chimu Adventures specialises in affordable Antarctic cruises. G Adventures also offers entry-level trips.

THE TIMING

The Antarctic cruising season goes from November until late March or early April. Most ships make an 11- or 12-day round trip on an all-inclusive basis. While the weather might be more unpredictable in those early and late months, November and March are the ideal times to find discount fares.

ROAD TRIP USA

The ultimate way to
experience the USA:
by car

The old **pick-up truck** rumbles down the street, a set of bull horns fixed to its faded bonnet.

A cigarette is drooping from the driver's mouth, and his wide-brimmed hat is clamped on tight. As the car rolls past it reveals a bumper sticker on the back: 'I killed a six-pack, just to watch it die.' That's probably not all this guy has killed. The original owner of those horns would be a candidate. And maybe an errant cowboy or two. Eventually the truck pulls away and the rumble fades, and it's all quiet again on the western front.

There's only one busy street in the town of Beatty, Nevada, and right now there's not a soul on it. It's lunchtime, and the few inhabitants of this tiny outpost are eating sandwiches at KC's Saloon. The sun beats down hard as folks talk about farmin' and huntin', while a few passersby talk mostly about drivin'.

See, you have to drive a long way to get to Beatty, Nevada. You have to drive down arrow-straight highways that cut through the endless desert, past ghost towns and places that look like they're only a couple of abandonments away from welcoming ghouls. There are boarded-up windows in these parts, old RVs rusting away in yards, waist-high weeds growing in old drive-in theatres.

This is the Wild, Wild West. The far west of the United States, frontier country, an arid and unforgiving land, a place of cowboys and their 'floozies', of hats on heads and six-shooters on hips, of old mining towns, haunted hotels, weather-beaten local faces, cold beer and a warm welcome.

Whether you're travelling solo or not, there's only one way to see the Wild West, and that's with a road trip. That's how I got here to Beatty, the halfway point on my solo Wild West adventure, a road journey that will take me from the historic town of Virginia City in the north of Nevada to the lights and glamour of Las Vegas in the south.

There's so much history and mythology in this area, so much of the way the US used to be, a side of the States you'll never find in the big cities. I've chosen to hit all of Nevada's old mining towns on this itinerary, keeping drive times short – no more than three or four hours a day – and exploration times long. Virginia City makes a natural jumping-off point for the Wild West, as one of Nevada's oldest and most successful gold-rush settlements, and Vegas is the ideal place to end, a hit of modernity after so many roadhouses and saloons.

I began at Gold Hill Hotel, an old place perched next to a former gold mine, where a fire trapped and killed 37 miners way back in the late 1800s. The hotel is now supposed to be haunted and it certainly becomes ominous once my fireplace settles to embers and the light in my room turns to inky black. Every bump in the night sounds grotesquely magnified when you're sleeping in a haunted house.

The sun rises the next day, however, and my road trip begins. The first part of the drive is on Highway 50, named 'The World's Loneliest Road' by the American Automobile Association. There's barely a soul out here – just tarmac, fresh air, an endless blue sky, and the sound of spinning wheels.

Four hours down dead-straight highways and I've finally reached Tonopah, another mining town that blossomed back in the early 1900s, with the discovery of silver. Tonight I'm staying at the Mizpah Hotel, a 107-year-old establishment that bore witness to Tonopah's glory days. The main elevator door still has a bullet hole in it.

The next day I'm tackling two hours of flat, straight highway down to Beatty, the one-horse cowboy town with no visible horse, but plenty of cowboys.

'Oh, the cowboys and the floozies will be out tonight,' says Debbie, who works at the town's Chamber of Commerce. 'They'll be wearin' their cowboy clothes, and you know why that is? Cos they ain't changed in a hundred years!'

She's right, too – they *are* wearing their cowboy clothes. That night at KC's Saloon I relax at the bar with a beer while guys with six-shooters on their hips work their way through a karaoke repertoire that takes in the two most popular types of music around here: country, and western.

Next day I've crossed the state border into California, going from the high plains of Beatty to the low, low depths of Death Valley. I explore this rocky, barren national park before climbing back into Nevada and onwards to Pahrump, a large town of weatherboard houses and glittering casinos, where the most popular restaurant on Yelp is also a brothel. I spend the night at a casino before hitting the road once again, driving down straight roads that become ever busier until I round a corner in the hills and there, laid out on the valley floor below, is Las Vegas. Civilisation. Another version of the Wild, Wild West.

If road trips are your thing, the USA is a country that was made for driving, and it's definitely something you can do on your own. The locals are friendly. The roads are good. And the scenery is magnificent. You can't go too wrong. ●

Bottom left: The Nevadan
ghost town of Rhyolite –
one of many former
mining towns left to ruin

Right: Amargosa Desert,
seen from Beatty

THE HIGHLIGHTS

If you choose to do your road trip through the Wild West, your highlights will likely be the interactions you have with the locals, with people who look like throwbacks to movies starring Clint Eastwood, all long coats and pistols on hips. History lives in Nevada. The roads might be modern and the car you're driving flash, but everything else will feel like a time warp until you hit Las Vegas.

In fact, the locals will probably be the stand-out of any drive in the US. Road trips tend to take you away from the popular tourist spots and into places where foreign accents aren't often heard, where solo travellers are a curiosity rather than a pain. Whether you drive the coast of California, the windy back roads of New England, the marshlands of the south or even tackle Route 66 in its entirety, you'll see beautiful scenery and have fun behind the wheel, but mostly you'll meet people, lots of people, strange, funny and interesting people, and they will find you fascinating.

THE DANGERS

If you're hitting the road in Nevada – or indeed in many of the western states of the US – there will be vast sections of open space, which means you need to be prepared. Carry plenty of water. Get a local SIM card for your phone so you can make calls and use the GPS. Have a plan in mind in case you break down. The driving itself is fairly safe, as US roads are good and traffic is predictable, so your main concerns will be the same as if you were travelling in any other way. Be aware of your surroundings, particularly in new cities, ask around about any security risks, don't pick up hitchhikers, and always lock your car doors while driving.

THE TRAVEL PLAN

Hiring a car isn't the cheapest way to get around, but it can be affordable. First of all, hunt through the internet for any deals or specials from reputable hire-car companies. It's also worth bearing in mind that if you do a circular trip, dropping your car off from the same place you picked it up, it will be cheaper than going from A to B. For an even cheaper alternative, look into car relocations. The travel website Transfercar has deals on moving rental cars from one city to another – perfect if you're travelling alone and are flexible with your itinerary.

THE TIMING

To replicate my trip through the Wild West of Nevada, allow yourself a week to ten days. The timeline for any other journey is completely up to you – you could take a few days, or a few years. And, though you can drive in the US at any time of year, it's worth remembering that the country has defined seasons, and some places in the south will be extremely hot in summer (June–August), while others in the north will be very cold, with ice and snow on the roads, in winter (December–February).

LA PAZ
TO LIMA

One of the most
famous views in
the world: Machu
Picchu, the Incan
ruins in Peru

Make sure you get a **window** seat.

Because as amazing as this part of South America is, as exciting and exotic and strange as this journey will be once you're on the ground, there's no better introduction to it than the view of La Paz from an aeroplane window.

Look down. The Andean Altiplano is flat and featureless for miles on approach, but suddenly it splits into a deep ravine, a valley that funnels down to the base of jagged snow-capped peaks on the far horizon. It takes a while to realise that all sides of that ravine are covered in houses – shabby brick structures that begin at the lip of the Altiplano and tumble down to the valley floor. There are high-rise buildings down there, too. There are brightly painted buses on the roads that connect them, cars blocking every inch of bitumen, people rushing up and down the steep inclines.

You catch a small flash of this as the plane banks and makes its way towards the runway at La Paz airport. And then you're in South America. Real South America. The best of it. This is your introduction to one of the world's great journeys, a trip that will take you through ancient civilisations, through wonders of the world, through cultures modern and traditional. It will cross soaring mountain peaks and barren plains, through some of the strangest,

most beautiful and most amazing sights you've ever seen. La Paz to Lima. The Incas to the Moche. Witchdoctors to coca growers. Guinea pigs to fine dining.

For solo travellers, this is how you should see South America. It's a well-trodden backpacker route, with good infrastructure and plenty of transport options, as well as big-ticket attractions like the Inca Trail, Machu Picchu and Lake Titicaca, but it also has that air of mystery, that feel of being out of your comfort zone in a foreign place.

La Paz is the perfect jumping-off point. It's big and it's busy and it's different. Its streets are choked with traffic 24 hours a day. It's charmless in some ways, fascinating in others. Shady characters call to you from dark corners. Witchdoctors peddle trinkets for good luck and bad. Skyscrapers abut Spanish colonial ruins. Street vendors sell unrecognisable food. It's bizarre and amazing.

Tourists come here to cycle the Death Road, the mountain track that clings to a cliffside nearby and has undone countless commuters in the past. They also come here to scale one of the nearby snowy peaks, or to just relax and get acclimatised to the altitude, and the attitude.

Bolivians, you find, march to the beat of their own drum. Women still wear bowler hats and woollen shawls. There's a church in the town of Copacabana that people visit to have their new cars blessed, because they say it's cheaper than buying insurance. There seem to be constant marches on city streets in either protest or celebration – sometimes it's hard to tell which.

And then you move on, and the journey only becomes more interesting. You cross the border at Lake Titicaca and enter Peru. Peru is similar, but different. There are remnants of some of the world's great civilisations here: the Incas, the Chimú, the Moche, the Nazca. The people of the high Andes have a completely different culture from those in the coastal lowlands. Cities like Cuzco are all about history and tradition; Lima, meanwhile, is all about modernity and creativity, from its high-end restaurants to its pumping bar scene.

All of this awaits. And it begins with the view from a plane seat. •

Top: Victor, a local Andean shaman, prays to the mountain gods for safe passage on the Salkantay Trail, Peru

Bottom: Hikers rest in the shadow of Salkantay mountain

Want to tackle this one totally solo? You can.

THE HIGHLIGHTS

Where do you begin? Well, in La Paz, obviously. Ride the Death Road — otherwise known as Yungas Road — on a mountain bike, if you dare. Tour the witches' markets. Eat salteñas, the Bolivian-style empanadas. And then move on, on a route that will become very obvious once you join all of the big-attraction dots. The next stop will be Copacabana, the lakeside town that provides access to Isla del Sol and Isla de la Luna, islands that are home to Incan ruins. Near Puno, also on the shores of Lake Titicaca, people still live on islands woven entirely from reeds.

You're now in Peru, where you can spend a good amount of time soaking up the charms of Cuzco, the ancient Incan capital and former Conquistador stronghold. Explore Machu Picchu, watch condors soar in Colca Canyon, before finally moving down from the Andean highlands towards the coast, stopping to take a flight over the Nazca

Lines, the huge and mysterious shapes carved into the desert floor by an ancient civilisation. Finally you arrive in Lima, bustling, intimidating Lima. Head to hipster Barranco to drink at trendy bars, or hang out in modern Miraflores for some of the world's finest food. And toast a truly great experience.

THE DANGERS

There are, unfortunately, security risks involved in tackling a trip like this on your own. South America is not 100 per cent safe, and Lima in particular has a reputation for petty theft and occasional violent crime. Solo travellers are more susceptible. You want to keep a low profile on a trip like this, which means wearing old clothes, not putting expensive camera gear on display, keeping watch over your belongings at all times, travelling on public transport only by day, and learning some basic Spanish phrases in order to not look like the total gringo you are. These destinations aren't inherently dangerous, but they do require more precautions than some others.

THE TRAVEL PLAN

Want to tackle this one totally solo? You can. For sure. Buses in Bolivia that are rated either 'cama' – with reclining seats – or 'semi-cama' – with semi-reclining seats – will be modern and comfortable. The same goes in Peru, where buses can go from economico, which are basic but fine, all the way up to luxury services with lie-back seats and waiter services. Peru also

has a reliable rail system in the high Andes. For those who want safety in numbers, there are also plenty of great tour companies that travel from La Paz to Lima, or vice versa, and have the added benefit of organising your Inca Trail permit (the numbers of which are strictly limited and need to be booked well in advance). Intrepid Travel has a great 22-day itinerary, and Tucan Travel also does a budget-friendly 14-day trip.

THE TIMING

If you're hoping to hike the Inca Trail, you'll need to be in Cuzco between April and October, though the area gets very busy in June and July. If you arrive in those months, it's worth looking into an alternative trek – for example, the Salkantay Trail is equally spectacular, and will take you close to Machu Picchu, but with only a fraction of the crowds. Regardless of your trekking desires, December to April is rainy season in the high Andean areas of Bolivia and Peru, so it's best to do this trip in the middle of the year (but bring warm clothes, as the nights get cold). Allow yourself a good three to four weeks to make your way from La Paz to Lima, though you could easily devote more if you wanted.

Opposite top: A llama stops for a quick feed on Isla del Sol, Bolivia

Opposite bottom: Plaza de Armas, the main square in La Paz, Bolivia

HO CHI MINH CITY TO HANOI

A scooter means complete freedom in Vietnam

You'll experience
Vietnam, real Vietnam,
and you'll feel a part of it.

Have I made a **terrible** mistake?

That is a question you will most definitely ask yourself at some point on your Vietnamese scooter adventure. That and other teasers like: was this the worst idea I've ever had? And should I turn around and just forget this whole thing ever happened? They're reasonable queries, and all of them flashed through my mind, the thoughts fighting their way through the chaos of noise and dust and bright lights that is central Ho Chi Minh City, about two minutes into my journey around Vietnam. Have I made a terrible mistake? Possibly.

I'd pulled out of the hire place on a 110cc Honda Blade, tootled down a quiet suburban street, and then emerged onto one of the main thoroughfares of this heaving metropolis. The enormity of my challenge was suddenly laid bare – and loud: the trucks that take no prisoners; the cars that stop and start and swerve with no warning; and the scooters, so many scooters, that dodge and weave through traffic, appearing out of nowhere from the side of the road, joining and leaving the vast torrent of traffic like twigs thrown around a raging river.

It's intimidating out there for first-timers. It's scary. A case could be made that it's also unnecessarily dangerous. But here's the thing you eventually learn – that I eventually learned – about riding a scooter by yourself around Ho Chi Minh City, and greater Vietnam, and in fact anywhere in South-East Asia: it's great. It's truly great. It doesn't have to be a white-knuckle hell ride, either. In fact, if you take the right precautions and allow yourself the time and space to ease into the rhythm of rural Asia, life on a scooter in Vietnam is one of the most rewarding, enjoyable solo travel experiences you can have.

It just takes a while to settle in – to get used to Vietnamese traffic conditions, Vietnamese speeds. At first glance the traffic in this country looks like it moves at breakneck pace, but the reality is it's actually quite slow. The national speed limit is 60 kilometres (37 miles) per hour. You very rarely even make it up that high. Most driving in Vietnam is done at a doddle, stuck as you are in choked streets trying to avoid a million other scooters and buses and trucks and cars.

The best of Vietnam lies by the side of those streets. The Vietnam you really want to see, the truly different and fascinating side to the country, is not accessible by train, or by bus. The only way you'll experience it, the only way to taste and smell and see it, is by getting around the same way pretty much everyone else in this country does: by motorbike or scooter.

You don't even have to ride that motorbike or scooter yourself. In fact, if you don't have any experience as a rider I would very much advise against it. There are still ways to make this trip happen on two wheels, which I've listed on page 245.

For now, though, let's concentrate on the experience of travelling from Vietnam's tip to its tail on two motorised wheels. You only have to force your way past the outskirts of the big cities to discover what's so great about exploring this land by scooter. The scenery is classic South-East Asia, all rice paddies and forested mountains, and small villages dwarfed by storm clouds that gather on the horizon each evening.

You see few tourists outside Vietnam's banana pancake trail, the well-established route that takes in Ho Chi Minh City, beachy Nha Trang, historic Hoi An, the old capital of Hue and the majesty of Halong Bay. There's so much in the areas that connect those dots, in the villages and towns, places where they barely ever see a foreigner, where on your little scooter you will be welcomed and stared at. You'll sleep each night in basic guesthouses, and start your mornings with noodle soup from the local market; you'll stop frequently for roadside iced coffees and breaks in hammocks.

The roads will make sense, after a while. The ducking and weaving through traffic will feel normal. The sight of a family of five all crowded onto one scooter won't even make you blink. You'll experience Vietnam, real Vietnam, and you'll feel a part of it. ●

THE HIGHLIGHTS

The main highlight of travelling from Ho Chi Minh City to Hanoi is the travel itself, the experience of exploring this country by scooter and really getting to know it. There are some unlikely pleasures out there, from the market-fresh meals to the stares from locals as you pull up next to them in the queue for a car ferry, or roll into a small village and start asking around for somewhere to stay. Though it makes sense to hug the coast here and enjoy all of the beaches and resorts, there's beauty and tranquillity in the central highlands, around areas like Dalat, as well as to the south-west of Ho Chi Minh, deep in the Mekong Delta.

Of the more obvious stops, Nha Trang is backpacker heaven, and the perfect spot to get back in touch with Western civilisation with a few boozy nights at tourist-friendly bars. Hoi An is similarly popular, and for good reason: you'd stop here for the heritage-listed old town, but you'd also stop just for the world's best banh mi, or pork rolls (check out Madam Khanh's for the absolute finest). Danang has nice beaches, Hue has the history, and Hanoi is a heady blend of Asian bustle and French colonial charm. And your scooter will always be your best friend.

THE DANGERS

Riding a motorbike or scooter is inherently dangerous in any country, let alone Vietnam. If safety is a big priority for you – and it should be – there are several things to think about before embarking on a trip like this, and the first is whether you have experience as a rider. If you don't, I would counsel against doing this trip on your own. Go with one of the other options listed opposite.

If you do want to ride, though, you'll need protective gear, and you'll want to bring your own stuff. Western-quality helmets aren't generally available in South-East Asia. Same goes with good riding gloves or boots.

You'll also need travel insurance, and you'll want to check the wording of your policy carefully. Some insurers won't cover you for motorbike trips. Others will only cover you if you are licensed to ride a motorbike back home, and are wearing a helmet when you ride. In Vietnam, licensing laws are murky and not always enforced – however, technically you need a Vietnamese licence to be 100 per cent legal. You won't be able to get one of these, which means you'll be at the mercy of any police officer who decides to pull you over.

You'll also need to consider the sort of bike you're renting, or buying. In Vietnam you can get a short-term rental from a company such as Tigit Motorbikes (www.tigitmotorbikes.com) or, for journeys longer than a month, you can buy a bike outright from the company and they'll buy it back from you at the end of the trip.

Breakdowns happen: A mechanic conducts running repairs on a motorbike outside Dalat

THE TRAVEL PLAN

If you don't want to ride your own motorbike through Vietnam, Easy Riders (www.dalat-easyrider.com.vn) is a company that provides motorbikes and experienced drivers, and itineraries through the country. All you have to do is strap your luggage on the back, climb on and hang on. Easy Riders began in Dalat, and has since been copied by numerous other companies, which go by such variations on the name as 'Easy Riders Vietnam', 'Vietnam Easy Riders', 'Original Easy Rider Vietnam', 'Vietnam Easy Riders Tours', and so on.

If you don't like the idea of motorbikes at all, then make your way from Ho Chi Minh to Hanoi by public transport. Vietnamese trains are reliable, if not super comfortable, and the bus service is cheap and easy to use. There are plenty of tour companies that travel this well-trodden route too.

THE TIMING

Be warned: this is a long trip. More than 1000 kilometres (621 miles). If you don't have at least a few months up your sleeve, do just part of it. Cruise around the northern highlands. Explore the Mekong Delta. Hang out on the central beaches. Wherever you choose to go, avoid monsoon season, because you're on a scooter, and being caught in the rain sucks. For the best weather, aim to travel between March and August. For more great info and suggested itineraries for motorbike trips in Vietnam, check out the website www.vietnamcoracle.com.

CONCLUSION

GO YOUR OWN WAY

You can do this.

Not only that: you *should* do this. Everyone should travel alone, at least once in their lives. That, I hope, is the knowledge and the inspiration that you've taken from this book. Travelling solo isn't a last resort and it isn't some sort of punishment. It's the ultimate adventure. It's the archetypal travel experience – raw and pure.

Everything is up to you now. The places you go, the things you see, the people you meet and the experiences you take with you for the rest of your life: they're all in your hands. They're all under your control.

Sure, the world may still seem an intimidating place when you first set off alone, a place filled with unpredictability and danger. But you should realise by now that it's also brimming with adventure – places, people and experiences all out there just waiting for you. And you have what it takes to explore and find them and to love every moment.

You can make new friends in new cities; you can find your way around strange places. You can cope with disaster, you can deal with disappointment, and you can embrace everything that makes this pursuit so amazing: the freedom, the adventure, the chance to get out there and discover who you really are and what you really want to do. Trust me: you will never forget this experience.

So, enjoy going your own way. Get out there and explore the world under your own steam. Change your plans at the last minute, say yes to unexpected opportunities, put yourself in the path of chance encounters that will change your life forever. Live the highs and the lows and take the lessons you learn along the way on to your next adventure, and the adventures after that. Marvel at the richness of the world there for your discovery, and at your own independence and capability and courage.

You'll never look back. ●

Exploring the high pathways of First, in central Switzerland

HANDY REFERENCES

The websites you'll need to plan, book and execute your solo journey

INSPIRATION

Accuweather: All the seasonal weather in your destination so you can decide on a good time to travel.
accuweather.com

Google Maps: Essential tool for plotting your itinerary.
maps.google.com

Instagram: Allows travellers to search travel photos using hashtags and geotags and follow other adventurers to gain inspiration.
instagram.com

Matador Network: Huge travel resource showcasing writers from around the world.
matadornetwork.com

Rome 2 Rio: Will tell you the fastest and best way to get to your destination.
rome2rio.com

Travelfish: A wealth of information on travel in South-East Asia.
travelfish.org

TripAdvisor: Global beast with millions of reviews of pretty much everything, which occasionally need to be taken with a grain of salt.
tripadvisor.com

Viator: Booking site for activities and experiences that can serve as great inspiration.
viator.com

Wikitravel: Crowd-sourced travel info that provides a different view from the mainstream industry.
wikitravel.com

Wikivoyage: Similar to Wikitravel.
wikivoyage.com

FLIGHTS

Adioso: The ideal site for those with a flexible itinerary, as it will find not only the cheapest airlines, but also the cheapest times to fly.
adioso.com

Flight Aware: Useful once you've booked, this site tracks flights and warns you about delays.
flightaware.com

Google Flights: The simplest flight aggregator to use, given you just need to google your route, and the flight options (with prices) will appear in your search results.
google.com/flights

Kayak: Another great aggregator that can quote fares by splitting carriers (say, fly Qantas to Singapore and then Lufthansa to Frankfurt), helping you find the cheapest flights.
kayak.com

Skyscanner: Flight aggregator with a huge range of airlines, making it very useful for research.
skyscanner.com

STA Travel: Good for discount flights for students and backpackers.
statravel.com.au

ACCOMMODATION

Airbnb: The world leader for short-term apartment rentals and house shares, and also has a large range of 'experiences' curated by locals in various cities.
airbnb.com

Couchsurfing: Facilitator that allows travellers to sleep for free on locals' couches, in their spare rooms or on their lounge room floors.
couchsurfing.com

Expedia: Hotel aggregator that can be handy for researching budget options.
expedia.com

Global Freeloaders: A worldwide network of free accommodation, similar to Couchsurfing.
globalfreeloaders.com

Hostelworld: The ultimate resource for researching and booking hostels around the world.
hostelworld.com

TrustedHousesitters: Allows you to stay in some beautiful homes for free, once you register.
trustedhousesitters.com

TOURS

Acacia Africa: Leaders in overland travel in Africa.
acacia-africa.com

Busabout: Hop-on, hop-off bus tours of Europe, plus epic party sailing trips.
busabout.com

Chimu Adventures: Specialists in affordable Antarctic cruises, as well as South American itineraries.
chimuadventures.com

Contiki: The original backpacker coach tours, with a range of destinations and travel styles.
contiki.com

G Adventures: Another excellent small-group adventure company.
gadventures.com.au

Intrepid Travel: World leaders in small-group adventure travel.
intrepidtravel.com

On The Go: Great group tours in a variety of locations.
onthegotours.com

Oz Experience: Backpacker-focused bus trips around Australia.
ozexperience.com

Singles Travel Connections: Small-group tours for solo travellers, with no single supplement.
singlestravel.com.au

Topdeck: Trips through Europe, Asia and North America for 18–30-somethings.
topdeck.travel

Tucan Travel: Affordable, fun tours in South and Central America.
tucantravel.com

Two's a Crowd: Tours and holidays for solo travellers.
twosacrowd.com.au

Urban Adventures: Specialists in single-day tours around the world.
urbanadventures.com

TRANSPORT

BlaBlaCar: Carpooling app that will put you in touch with people going your way.
blablacar.com

Drive Now: The best deals on hire cars around the world.
drivenow.com.au

Eurail: Offers discount European rail passes for non-EU citizens.
eurail.com

InterRail: Discounted European rail passes for those from the EU.
interrail.eu

Lyft: Great ride-sharing app for the USA.
lyft.com

Taxify: Competitor to Uber offering similar service.
taxify.eu

The Man in Seat 61: Invaluable resource for anyone travelling by train.
seat61.com

Uber: Ride-sharing app that works in pretty much every city.
uber.com

FOOD

Eater: Restaurant reviews and foodie news from around the world.
eater.com

Migrationology: Great food/travel blog written by a passionate and knowledgeable foodie.
migrationology.com

OpenTable: Booking site for restaurants across the globe.
opentable.com

Serious Eats: Food blog stacked with info for eating in thousands of destinations.
seriouseats.com

Time Out: Has great restaurant reviews in selected cities.
timeout.com

FINDING WORK

GoOverseas: Solid info on studying, working and interning abroad.
gooverseas.com

Teach Away: Lists teaching jobs all over the world.
teachaway.com

TEFL: Offers the qualifications to teach English, as well as job opportunities.
tefl.com

Workaway: Allows travellers to volunteer in exchange for food and board.
workaway.info

WWOOF: Worldwide opportunities to volunteer and work on organic farms.
wwoofinternational.org

FINDING FRIENDS

A Small World: A paid-subscription travel and social network, putting like-minded travellers together.
asmallworld.com

Backpackr: Social app that hooks you up with nearby travellers.
backpackr.org

Meetup: Helps travellers meet up with fellow adventurers in a variety of locations around the world.
meetup.com

Social media apps (various): The likes of Instagram, Snapchat, Facebook and WhatsApp are essential for staying in touch with new friends.

Twitter: The micro-blogging site aids in connecting with new friends and attending meet-ups.
twitter.com

SAFETY/ADVICE

BSafe: Personal safety app that allows you to create a network of contacts who will be alerted in case of emergency.
getbsafe.com

Smart Traveller: Australian government travel advisory with bulletins and up-to-date safety information on various countries.
smartraveller.gov.au

UK Foreign Office: Travel advice from the British government.
gov.uk/foreign-travel-advice

US Department of State: Travel advisory for US citizens.
state.gov/travel

About the author

Ben Groundwater is a travel writer, photographer and broadcaster whose work has been published across the globe. He is the author of two travel books, writes weekly columns for the *Sydney Morning Herald* and *The Age*, hosts the popular travel podcast "Flight of Fancy", and has twice been named the Australian Society of Travel Writers' "Travel Writer of the Year". He lives in Sydney, though his heart belongs in San Sebastian, Spain.

Find out more at bengroundwater.com

Acknowledgements

I owe a huge debt of gratitude to the whole team at Hardie Grant, without whom this project would never have been possible. To Melissa Kayser, Megan Cuthbert, Emma Schwarz, Vanessa Masci, Eugenie Baulch and everyone else who had a hand in making *Go Your Own Way* a reality, thank you.

I'd also like to thank Anthony Dennis, Craig Platt and Jane Reddy at Fairfax Traveller for their continued support; and my agent, Pippa Masson, for all of her hard work.

A brief but heartfelt shout-out, too, to all of the characters who are mentioned in this book, all of the people I've met on my solo adventures who have provided so much inspiration and enjoyment over the years. You guys are the reason I love to travel. Thank you.

And finally, I'm saving the biggest thanks of all for my live-in editor, the sounding board for my half-baked ideas, the voice of reason when I need one, the fierce defender when I don't, the mother of my child, the love of my life, and the perfect travel companion, Jess. Here's to many more years going our own way.

Published in 2019 by Hardie Grant Travel,
a division of Hardie Grant Publishing

Hardie Grant Travel (Melbourne)
Building 1, 658 Church Street
Richmond, Victoria 3121

Hardie Grant Travel (Sydney)
Level 7, 45 Jones Street
Ultimo, NSW 2007

www.hardiegrant.com/au/travel

A catalogue record for this book is available from the National Library of Australia

Go Your Own Way
ISBN 9781741176438

10 9 8 7 6 5 4 3 2 1

Publisher
Melissa Kayser

Project editor
Megan Cuthbert

Editors
Emma Schwarcz and Eugenie Baulch

Editorial assistance
Rosanna Dutson and Aimee Barrett

Design
Vanessa Masci

Typesetting
Kerry Cooke

Prepress
Kerry Cooke and Splitting Image Colour Studio

Printed in China by 1010 Printing International Limited